dfree® Lifestyle

12 STEPS TO FINANCIAL FREEDOM

SAY YES TO NO DEBT

2nd Edition

DeForest B. Soaries, Jr.

FAITH-BASED WORKBOOK

Published by DBS Solutions

dfree® Lifestyle: 12 Steps to Financial Freedom Say Yes To No Debt Workbook 2nd Edition has been written, compiled, and edited by DeForest B. Soaries, Jr.

Library of Congress Cataloging in Publication data

ISBN-13: 978-1-7356124-6-1

1. Financial Information 2. Christian living

Cover design: Benny Goodman

Printed in the United States of America

A Note from DeForest B. Soaries, Jr.

Welcome to the **dfree®** lifestyle workbook! This workbook is designed for you to use as a companion to my book, ***Say Yes to No Debt: 12 Steps to Financial Freedom***. I am thrilled you have decided to join me in a personal journey to financial freedom. The 12 steps I describe in this workbook represent the same 12 steps I took many years ago to address my personal financial situation. It is an honor to share my story and my strategy with you.

Our motto is "Say Yes to No Debt." Our foundational Bible verse is Proverbs 22:7 (NIV): "The rich rule over the poor; and the borrower is slave to the lender."

Because we live in a consumer-driven culture, it is imperative that Christian consumers have the knowl- edge and support needed to be healthy and mature consumers. Fortunately, you recognize that you could use some help in the area of personal finance. I am thrilled to take this journey with you and offer you the tools needed.

And that is what this workbook is — a tool. My goal is that you will discover more about yourself than you do about money by the time you complete this experience. That is why I call it the **dfree®** lifestyle. I never learned to manage money. What I did learn was to manage my life and then use money to reach my goals. That is what this workbook is designed to help you accomplish also.

I created and started using the term "**dfree®**" in 2005 when I began helping people address and conquer the greatest barrier to stress-free living and wealth creation: personal debt. The principles **dfree®** represents are very simple:

No debt: Pay as we go — use cash and debit cards rather than credit cards. Live without debt.
No delinquencies: Pay bills on time — avoid late payments and late fees.
No deficits: Live below our means — spend less than we earn.

These three principles translate into financial wellness and the money we "find" creates a path toward wealth creation. The results of the **dfree®** lifestyle will surprise you! I have seen thousands of people change their lives and their families' futures when they "Say Yes to No Debt." And it gets easier as the journey unfolds!

Of course, the **dfree®** lifestyle is easier said than done. Achievement of **dfree®** goals has less to do with information and more to do with your values, habits, attitudes, perspectives, and relationships. So here we go: from debt, delinquencies, and deficits to making Deposits into our own accounts, having Deeds for real estate, and earning Dividends from investments!

Visit **www.dfreefoundation.org** for more information.

Thank you for allowing me to join you in your **dfree®** journey!

DeForest B. Soaries, Jr.

Understanding Your Workbook

The following is a brief introduction to the contents of your workbook. These steps are designed to be taken as you read through the **dfree®** book. Each lesson is divided into six sections and includes the following elements:

I. THE JOURNEY BEGINS:

- Opening Prayer: This is a suggested prayer based on the content presented in the lesson. It can be replaced by a personal or group prayer as desired.
- Response: This is a brief statement that affirms one principle associated with the **dfree®** lifestyle and the next leg of the journey. It is designed to create the mindset that enhances the content.
- Life Situation: Short stories that reveal financial and other related issues connected to issues and topics that happen within our lives. There are statements or questions for you to complete that ad- dress the situation in the story and may apply to your personal finances or situation.

II. UNCOVERING THE CHAINS:

Our Session's Goal: This section is what the lesson is about and the intended outcome of each lesson.

Memory Verse: This should be memorized at the beginning of each step. This reinforces the idea that the practical **dfree®** strategies are all based on Biblical principles. There is space available to write a reflection if you think the Scripture applies to your life today and how.

A Financial Stronghold Message From Dr. Soaries: This narrative is my message to you that builds on the points made in the **dfree®** book. It is designed to motivate you to continue making progress toward your goal.

Barriers or Obstacles: Those things which keep us from moving forward in our financial (and other areas) freedom.

Scripture and Practical Living: Scripture verse(s) that is applicable to the **dfree®** principals and pro- vides support to help you work through your obstacles.

III. BEGINNING TO BREAK AND ELIMINATE THE FINANCIAL CHAINS:

Review Key Terms: Terms from the lesson you will want to know much more about.

Suggestion Box: This is a reminder to use the Key Terms and create an activity using the terms. Information and Statistics: Interesting facts and figures related to the lesson material.

Activity and Exercises: A short story highlighting the goal with questions or statements to complete.

dfree® Affirmation: These are three beliefs that offer you words of encouragement as you work through your financial situation. They should be reflected upon carefully before proceeding if their meaning is not obvious.

IV. VICTORY STORY:

V. COMMITMENTS AND ASSIGNMENT(S):

Discovery: This is where you pause to identify and document new discoveries that have occurred as a result of the **dfree®** lifestyle experience.

Commitments: This section invites you to make specific commitments to specific tasks prior to your next session. This is where the action and the change take place.

Benefits: Where you identify, in advance of your action, the benefits of doing what you have committed to do. By describing how you will benefit after completing the commitments, you will be encouraged to complete the tasks.

VI. HOME ASSIGNMENTS:

The reading assignment for the next session and a brief reflection assignment are included in this section.

Closing prayer: A suggested prayer to end your study. Please feel free to replace this suggested prayer with your own prayer.

Resources: Websites that will provide additional information and resources related to the lesson.

NOTES TO REMEMBER:

- This workbook is a tool and a guide. It is not intended to be a script or notes for a lecture. When using it to lead a class or small group, please be flexible and open to creative, interactive approaches that allow people to make the material their own. The workbook should be used as the basis for self-discovery and interaction among people who want to achieve financial freedom. Thank you for your help.

- All of the work you do using this workbook as your guide must be kept confidential. If you are involved in **dfree®** classes or a **dfree®** group, you will never be required to disclose any of your personal business. Your business should remain YOUR BUSINESS! Besides your spouse if you are married, the only people who should have access to your personal financial information are your attorney, accountant, financial planner, financial advisor, insurance agent, or other professionals with whom you have established a formal relationship.

- It is important to remember to proceed at your own pace. Many will decide to use this workbook during a 12-week period, but there is no time requirement for the "**dfree®** lifestyle" process. Just remember it does take time to change our behavior, and that is a significant aspect of this strategy.

- For additional resources and assistance, please visit our website: www.dfreefoundation.org.

The Story of Claude and Grace

Meet Claude and Grace. Claude, age 41, and Grace, age 39, have been married for 20 years. They have five children and are soon-to-be grandparents. Two of the children are twins. They were the children of Grace's sister Kara, and her brother-in-law, Chris. Kara and Chris were both killed in a car accident. Although they had been married for only a few years, Grace and Claude decided to adopt the twins. Many family members and friends said they would help and they kept their promise. Both of their parents are still living; Claude's parents are Garrett W. and Shirley R. Smith, and Grace's parents are Douglass T. and Harriett S. Boone. Claude and Grace live in a comfortable home, own a car, and enjoy traveling. Claude works for a worldwide delivery com- pany. His hobbies are sports—almost any sport—jazz music, and grilling. He works part-time at the church as a handyman and volunteers with the local community center's at-risk youth pro- gram on weekends. Grace is manager of a local grocery store a few blocks from their home and enjoys planning events and cooking for family and friends as well as football, basketball, swim- ming, traveling, and playing the drums. When the church drummer is away, Grace will step in and play the drums! She volunteers twice a month at the senior center, is a co-step leader of the local award-winning girl's step team, and is a member of both the church finance ministry and the community center's ski club. Claude and Grace both like to spend quality time with their family members and they pray together every day. They attend one intense Bible Study class each year, and are regular attendees of Sunday Bible School.

Claude and Grace are our guides as we experience the **dfree®** lifestyle. They will walk with us through the 12 steps in this workbook and share information about their journey towards financial freedom.

Claude and Grace are such active, energetic, and caring people that their story makes us wonder how they could be our guides toward financial freedom. On the surface, their lives seem to be fine and fun, yet everything that glitters on the outside may not be solid gold inside. Claude and Grace have had their share of problems—from marital issues to financial strangleholds. It took them more than a minute to break free from their struggles and break the bonds of financial debt. As we walk with Claude and Grace, maybe we can see our story in their story, or at least recognize someone we know through their journey.

Before you begin your journey toward financial freedom, pray, trust, and know that God will lead you through this endeavor. However, you—and you alone—must dedicate the time and effort to make a difference in your life and in the lives of others. Now let's get started!

Table of Contents

dfree® Lifestyle

LEVEL ONE – GET STARTED

STEP ONE – ADMIT THE PROBLEM

Opening prayer: *"Dear God, I am beginning a journey toward financial freedom. I pray You will give me the strength to see myself, to help myself, and to trust Your instructions. Thank You for what is about to happen in my life. Amen."*

Response: *Once I communicate and admit to myself that I have a financial problem, then I am more open to finding out the reasons and solutions to the problem.*

Life Situation – READ AND COMPLETE THE STORY BELOW: From Joy to Pain

Claude and Grace received their first credit cards in their senior year of college, respectively. Claude purchased items from food to sporting goods, and paid for gas sometimes when he needed a ride with some- one or went out with his friends. He was careful only to buy things he could pay off within two months. He had a part-time job at school and his parents would send him money once a month. Grace only paid for items she could afford.

After they were married, using their credit cards became a convenient way for Claude and Grace to meet their needs and have some wants as well. Repaying student loans also weighed heavily on them. Unfortunately, their ability to pay off their debts was not as timely. Their spending habits and lack of timely payments created....

____

____

Claude and Grace were no longer living as college singles when they entered into a life of bills, debt, responsibility, and choices.

When did you begin to allow debt to influence/control you?

____

____

I. UNCOVERING THE CHAINS

Our session today is about barriers. The goal of this session is to admit that we have financial challenges and discovering the barriers that must be removed in order to reach our financial target.

Memory Verse: "The rich rule over the poor, and the borrower is slave to the lender" (Proverbs 22:7, NIV).

Reflect and share with someone why you think Solomon said this. Are his words true in your life today and how?

____

____

A FINANCIAL STRONGHOLD MESSAGE FROM DR. SOARIES:

When I graduated from high school, my family bought me a used car that I planned to take to college. At first, I would drive all week after having bought only one dollar's worth of gas! Then I received a gas credit card in the mail. I started filling my tank every time I went to the gas station. My income had not increased (I had no income), but that card gave me more buying power. After one month, my gas credit card bill was $200. I made the minimum payment of $10 and that began a 15-year struggle with overspending, credit cards, and debt.

My story is similar to that of many Americans who are dealing with financial stress on a daily basis. The presence of overwhelming debt exists and is growing in every sector of American life. Not only is our nation drowning in debt, but American citizens have also become addicted to credit cards, high interest loans, and borrowing as a lifestyle. This means that we feel we simply cannot wait until we have the money to make certain purchases; that we cannot wait to obtain the things we want; that we are willing to pay high interest rates in return for the right to own items we cannot afford. This has become a national problem that seems to know no boundaries. We will never own businesses, be prepared for emergencies, or leave a legacy for the future if we are drowning in debt today. Getting out of debt is the first step toward financial freedom.

The ability to be content in any circumstance is a sure sign of spiritual maturity. The idea that I "must" have that tie or that suit or those shoes suggests that I cannot be content without them. It is precisely that "mentality" that causes us to use credit cards to buy those things we think give us our contentment. If we have that same relationship, we can have that same contentment and resist the feeling that we need things to make us happy.

Barriers or Obstacles: Those things or areas in my life that keep me financially strangled and financially indebted are (use the notes section in the back as necessary):

1.____

2.____

3.____

4.____

Scripture and Practical Living:

The Apostle Paul said this in his letter to the Philippians:

"...for I have learned to be content in any circumstance. I have experienced times of need and times of abundance. In any and every circumstance I have learned the secret of contentment, whether I go satisfied or hungry have plenty or nothing. I am able to do all things through the one who strengthens me" (Philippians 4:11-13 NIV).

For Paul, contentment came as a result of his relationship with Christ. Share how this Scripture is a support to you as you work through your barriers or obstacles.

____

____

II. BEGINNING TO BREAK AND ELIMINATE THE FINANCIAL CHAINS

Review Key Term(s):

Debt — something, usually money, owed by one party to another. (investopedia.com/terms/d/debt.asp)

SUGGESTION BOX **Highlight the Key Term(s) or create an activity using the Key Terms**

Information and Statistics:

- Americans have $5.1 trillion in consumer debt. This does not include mortgages. Mortgages are $12.04 trillion of the overall debt. The average U.S. household with debt carries $17,956 in credit card debt and $170,182 in total debt (nerd- wallet.com).
- Most U.S. adults have not reviewed their credit score (52 percent) or credit report (66 percent) in the past twelve months (National Foundation for Credit Counseling 2015).

This is sobering information about our lives personally and as a nation.

- Why do you think as a nation we have so much consumer debt?
- What are some reasons why people should review their credit score?
- Have you checked your score lately? Why or why not?

Activity and Exercises

Remember Claude and Grace, the young college love-is-all-we-need couple? Well, their "happy" lives began to change because of their financial choices and the arguing that began to shift the dynamics of their relationship, feelings, thoughts about one another, and maybe even them.

Let's do some investigating and see if we can find out what might be the cause of their problems and provide them with some solutions to help. By helping them, we may even help ourselves or someone else we know. Reread their story and answer the following. You can do this individually or in groups:

- List the financial barriers Claude and Grace have:

1.____

2.____

3.____

- Write two challenges you believe keep Claude and Grace in their financial situation:

1.____

2.____

- Create two financial goals for Claude and Grace:

1.____

2.____

Share your answers with the class. If you are working through the process by yourself, discuss with someone who is part of the **dfree®** ministry whom you trust or ask a close friend to review your response.

As I analyzed Claude and Grace's financial problems, I realized that I can provide help for others and apply this to myself. Maybe Claude, Grace, and I, (________ first name) can benefit from some positive changes in my actions, thoughts, and feelings. Therefore, I will repeat the dfree® Affirmation statements of encouragement to myself. (Look in the mirror and repeat the dfree® Affirmation statements.)

dfree® Affirmation	**1.** There is room for improvement in the way I handle my finances. **2.** There are resources available that can guide me to a better life. **3.** I will have to change the way I think if I am going to change the way I live.

III. ASSIGNMENT(S)

Read and complete the assignments before you begin the next session.

Discovery: I have discovered the following barriers are preventing me from achieving financial

(Check all that apply):

- ☐ Lottery tickets
- ☐ Car loans
- ☐ Family/friends
- ☐ Student loan
- ☐ Freedom
- ☐ Credit cards
- ☐ Payday loans
- ☐ Auto loans
- ☐ Auto title loans
- ☐ Gambling
- ☐ Other ____________________

____

____

____

____

Commitments: As a result of my discovery, I commit to the following actions:

Commitment #1: I will open an account that I do not currently have (circle all that apply):

1. Bank or credit union checking account
2. Bank or credit union savings account
3. Investment account
4. Retirement account
5. College savings account

Commitment #2: I will list three to five challenges I have had in the area of finances:

1. ____

2. ____

3. ____

4. ____

5. ____

Commitment #3: I will name at least three financial goals I have:

1. ____

2. ____

3. ____

4.____

5.____

6.____

Commitment #4: I am proud of these financial actions I have taken:

____

____

____

____

Commitment #5: I will identify and invite someone to join me in my **dfree®** journey:

Yes: ________ Date: _____/_____/_____

If I miss the date above, I will invite someone to join me in my **dfree®** journey on _____/_____/_____ (date).

Commitment #6: I will join the **dfree®** Billion Dollar Challenge (www.billiondollarpaydown.com) and set my personal debt reduction goals.

Date joined: _____/_____/_____ Please record login username and password for future reference.

Commitment #7: I will be ready for the next **dfree®** steps on _____/_____/_____.

Benefits: As a result of keeping my commitments, my life will be better in the following ways:

1.____

2.____

3.____

IV. VICTORY STORY

"Just a quick note to tell you how much I appreciate your guidance over the past 3 ½ years. It has changed my focus; I live within my means. I don't desire to purchase just because. I save more than 85% of the children's income. I pay myself first. I give to the church monthly and donate to help others. I have a will, disability insurance, and adequate life insurance.

My goals continue to concentrate on healthy mind, body, and living without debt, deficit, or delinquency. I use credit cards and pay them in full each month (no late fees, no annual fees, no finance charges). My taxes are current. My most recent credit score (which I will frame) is 733 (after credit fraud, which had me at 340 – I stayed focused and reaped the result without [the help of] an agency). These are just a few of my successes in the past 3 yrs. I'm so grateful for how I've been blessed in the midst of my adversity."

– B.C.

V. HOME ASSIGNMENT: Read chapter two, "Address the Mess" in the **dfree®** book.

Complete the following after you have had a moment to reflect on the class, your situation, and pray.

What responsible actions do I need to schedule and do this week:

____

____

____

____

Closing prayer: *"Thank You, God, for the victory I have experienced already. You are an awesome God and I commit this journey to You. I believe I can do this because I will depend on Your power to help me. Amen."*

Resources:

Bankrate.com

Federalreserve.gov

Mymoney.gov

Fdic.gov

dfree® Lifestyle

LEVEL ONE – GET STARTED

STEP TWO – ADDRESS THE MESS

Opening prayer: *"Dear God, I appreciate the fact that every new day You provide gives me an opportunity to experience new growth. Thank You for today and for this new opportunity. Amen."*

Response: If it is to be, it is up to me.

LIFE SITUATION – READ AND ANSWER THE QUESTION(S) BELOW: Frustrated and Tired

Another baby, another year, and more bills. Life was in full swing with no semester breaks. Grace was thankful and content being a mom and wife. Yet, she was tired of barely making ends meet. Claude did not seem as worried, Grace thought. They talked about their financial problems and other issues that worried them because of the finances, but Claude would always say, "Every- thing is going to be alright." Grace would always ask when and how. Claude would say he had things under control. They were both tired and frustrated from talking about this stuff, so they would leave the conversations feeling bad, but not having any real solutions. Grace's parents, Douglass and Harriett, noticed that she was withdrawn and quiet at times. They would ask her if something was wrong. Grace would smile and say, "I'm making it."

Grace's parents were concerned. Suggest how they can support Grace. What should Claude and Grace do about their situation?

___

___

___

I. UNCOVERING THE CHAINS

Our session today is about barriers. The goal of this session is to address our financial mess by addressing the barriers we have and by getting financially organized.

Memory Verse: "There is a way that seems right to man, but in the end it leads to death" (Proverbs 14:12, NIV).

Reflect and share with someone why you think Solomon said this. Are his words true in your life today and how?

____

____

A FINANCIAL STRONGHOLD MESSAGE FROM DR. SOARIES:

Let's go back to the barriers that prevent us from achieving financial freedom. How do we identify them? Often the biggest problem is the way we handle and spend money. The key word for spending is consumption.

There are three types of consumption that seem to describe the way we are handling money. First, there is what we call compensatory consumption. Compensatory spending is spending that we do when we are trying compensate for something missing in our lives that we believe we deserve. This is when we spend money to buy things that make us feel better about ourselves. It's when we spend money on things, but we are actually using the things we buy to compensate for a sense of unworthiness, disappointment, or sadness. When we do compensatory spending, we are really attempting to buy good feelings like happiness and significance.

We sometimes shop just to feel better. Some people call this "retail therapy." We live in a tough, competitive world. Everyday life has a way of making us feel less significant than we would like. And so subconsciously, we often spend money to gain the feeling of significance and happiness we fail to get from our relationships.

Second, there is the type of spending coined as conspicuous consumption. This type of spending happens when we use the attainment of things to gain status. I love to buy button-down collar shirts for $19.99. But there was a time when the shirts I purchased would all have a picture of a man riding a horse and holding a stick visibly positioned on the front – and the shirt would cost $59.99 instead of $19.99. Everything else about the shirt was the same ... except the picture. We call the picture a logo. One day I decided it did not make sense to spend $40 more on a shirt just to have a picture of a man on a horse holding a stick playing a game that I don't even understand. I have never been to a polo match in my life!

Too many of us have been convinced that our social status is achieved by spending money on things that cost more than they should. And many will spend substantially more for the famous or popular logo or brand because that image represents a certain status and level of success. That picture sends the message that I am in the know-that I have enough money to buy the shirt with the logo on it. And this behavior does not stop with shirts. Spending for status costs some people millions of dollars on items like houses, boats, cars, and jets.

Finally, there is what I call confused spending, which involves making purchases without stopping to think, analyze, or assess the cost or cost benefit of what we are actually getting for our money. It is confusing. How did a whole nation of people become addicted to a cup of coffee that costs more than $4 for a small cup? Are we that devoted to the coffee and its exotic names and flavors? Do we really feel better knowing we're drinking coffee that comes from Guatemala, Ethiopia, or anyplace else? When I was growing up, Chock full o'Nuts coffee was popular. It was known as the "heavenly coffee." But we weren't going to pay $4 or more for a cup of that coffee even if it had been made in heaven! Imagine what $4 a day, five days a week, for 50 weeks a year represents! $1,000. Yes – that's a thousand dollars!

If our status is sought through external things, it's no wonder we will spend money we don't have because we have to keep up with our own status. Some years ago, someone used the phrase "keeping up with the Joneses." Many of us aren't even trying to keep up with the Joneses - we're trying to keep up with ourselves. We see advertising images of other people and we have this picture in our heads that we become determined to make real – even if we cannot afford it.

Barriers or Obstacles: I have discovered that I have been influenced by advertising to practice:

1. Compensatory consumption when I purchased ______________________________.

2. Conspicuous consumption when I purchased ______________________________.

3. Confused consumption when I purchased ______________________________.

Scripture and Practical Living:

"Whoever gives heed to instruction prospers, and blessed is he who trusts in the Lord" (Proverbs 16:20, NIV).

Share how this Scripture is a support to you as you work through your barriers or obstacles.

____

____

II. BEGINNING TO BREAK AND ELIMINATE THE FINANCIAL CHAINS

Review Key Term(s):

Credit report – A credit score is a detailed breakdown of your credit history prepared by a credit bureau. Credit bureaus collect financial information about you and compile their reports based on that information. The three major credit bureaus – Equifax, Experian, and TransUnion – are each required to provide you with a free report at least once a year. (investopedia.com/terms/creditreport.asp)

Credit score – A credit score is a prediction of your credit behaviour, such as how like you are to pay a loan back on time, based on information from your credit reports. Companies use credit scores to make decisions on whether to offer you a mortgage, credit card, auto loan, and other credit products as well as for tenant screening and insurance. They are used to determine the interest rate and credit limit you receive. (consumerfinance.gov/ask-cfpb/what-is-a-credit-score-en-315/)

Compensatory spending – Compensatory spending is purchasing items to gain significance because of a person's feelings and thoughts of unworthiness.

Conspicuous spending (consumption) – Conspicuous spending (consumption) is purchasing things to gain status to elevate one's self or flaunting status.

Confused spending – Confused spending is when purchases are made without analyzing, thinking, or assessing the benefit or the cost of the item(s).

SUGGESTION BOX **Highlight the Key Term(s) or create an activity using the Key Terms**

Information and Statistics:

- Thirty-three percent of the population has at least two credit cards (creditcard.com 2014).
- People spend 12% - 18% more when using credit cards than using cash (Dunn and Bradstreet, nerdwallet.com).
  - What are some reasons why people should review their credit report?
  - Have you checked your score lately? Why or why not?

Activity and Exercises

Grace was frustrated. She knew she had to do something but she was not sure what to do. Claude was not helping. He did have some thoughts, but he was unsure about how to solve their problem. If Grace would stop bugging him, he knew that he could work it out. Claude did think of calling the debt-free number from the commercial he saw, but he also thought they should at least look at a new car first. He knew they had good enough credit for the car Grace had hinted at for months.

Let's do some investigating and see if we can find out what might be the cause of their problems and provide them with some solutions to help them. In helping them, we may even help ourselves or someone else we know. Reread their story and answer the following questions. You can do this individually or with others:

- List possible reasons why Grace and Claude can't talk through their financial problems:

1.____

2.____

3.____

- Write two challenges you believe keep Grace and Claude from moving to an honest conversation about money and spending:

1.____

2.____

- Create two financial goals for Claude and Grace:

1.____

2.____

Share your answers with the class. If you are working through the process by yourself, discuss with someone who is part of the **dfree®** ministry whom you trust or ask a close friend to review your response.

As I analyzed Claude and Grace's financial problems, I realized that I can provide help for others, and apply this to myself. Maybe Claude, Grace, and I, (_______ first name) can benefit from some positive changes in my actions, thoughts, and feelings. Therefore, I will repeat the dfree® Affirmation statements of encouragement to myself. (Look in the mirror and repeat the dfree® Affirmation statements.)

dfree® Affirmation

1. I can improve the way I handle my personal business.
2. It helps me to be challenged to take action.
3. I need to stop thinking about changing and actually do something.

III. VICTORY STORY

"My wife and I are both college educated, with good jobs, two cars, and a nice home. With four kids, two older and two younger, we have always used our credit cards to get by when something comes up. While we've known a lot of the basic financial information before, it didn't hit home until I lost my job due to a corporate downsizing and began to panic when I realized just how deep in consumer debt we had fallen. It felt like the weight of the world had fallen on my shoulders all at once.

A lot of the reasons we became so dependent on credit cards had nothing to do with money. We were trying to keep up with a standard of living that doesn't reflect our values or who we really are. I was fortunate to find another job fairly fast, and it even paid a little better than the one I lost. But how we approached our finances changed for good.

I'm happy to say that we're now on the road to being debt-free thanks to the principles of **dfree®**. For the first time in years, I don't dread paying the bills each month. The hardest part was getting started, but once you take the first step, then you can take another, and another, and soon you're on your way to a debt-free life."

- Doug S.

IV. COMMITMENTS AND ASSIGNMENT(S)

Review and complete the following assignments before you begin the next session.

Commitments: As a result of my discovery, I commit to the following actions:

Commitment #1: Much of our spending is influenced by advertising. I will track and translate the advertising messages I see today in the following chart (use additional paper):

FOR WHAT?	WHERE?	MESSAGES?
Ex. "X" brand deodorant	T.V. commercial	You will be significant or have statusif you use it.

Commitment #2: I will list three ways I can avoid being influenced by ads:

1.____

2.____

3.____

Commitment #3: I will conduct a financial snapshot "treasure hunt."

I will gather and read as many of my financial documents as I can, using the checklist below. Getting organized will help me understand my current financial standing. Once I have gathered and read these documents, I will identify any important issues and start a filing system to keep my financial documents organized and accessible.

- ☐ Pay stubs for the past month
- ☐ Annual income taxes withheld (W2s) and property taxes paid
- ☐ Public benefits paperwork

- ☐ Savings and investment account statements
- ☐ Retirement account statements—IRAs, 401(k)s, 403(b)s, pensions, etc.
- ☐ Monthly contribution amounts to savings/investment accounts
- ☐ Insurance premiums for auto, home, health, group plans, life
- ☐ Insurance policies, benefits, and distributions and/or recent statements
- ☐ Loan statements—home mortgage, installment loans, credit cards, etc.

- Company benefits statements
- General household expense information—food expenses, utilities, maintenance, etc.

Commitment #4: I will obtain a free copy of my credit report from one credit agency (Transunion, Experian, or Equifax) at www.annualcreditreport.com. (This will not include your credit score, but it will reveal important information about your accounts such as detecting that someone has stolen your identity and is using your name to apply for credit).

Commitment #5: I will make a list of all my sources of income:

1. ______
2. ______
3. ______
4. ______
5. ______
6. ______

Commitment #6: I will make a list of all my debt and ongoing bills:

DEBT (credit cards, student loans, auto loan, etc.)

1. ______
2. ______
3. ______
4. ______
5. ______
6. ______

ONGOING BILLS (rent, mortgage, utilities, transportation, insurance, etc.)

1.____

2.____

3.____

4.____

5.____

6.____

7.____

8.____

9.____

10.____

Commitment #7: I will attend the next **dfree®** session on _______ at________ .

Benefits: As a result of keeping my commitments, my life will be better in the following ways:

1.____

2.____

3.____

V. HOME ASSIGNMENT: Read chapter three, "Adjust the Attitude" in the dfree® book. Answer the following after you have had a moment to reflect on the class, your situation, and pray. Responsible Actions I need to schedule and do this week:

Closing prayer: *"God, I can feel myself getting stronger, getting better, and getting closer to where I need to be. My faith in You is causing me to take actions that will make me a better me. Amen."*

Resources:

Ownthedollar.com

Annualcreditreport.com

Consumerfinance.gov/credit-cards

Answers.com

dfree® Lifestyle

LEVEL ONE – GET STARTED

STEP THREE – ADJUST THE ATTITUDE

Opening prayer: *"Open my eyes, O God, that I may see. Amen."*

Response: My attitude is most important in determining my success.

LIFE SITUATION – READ AND ANSWER THE QUESTION(S) BELOW: I Want It Now!

Children can sometimes be very demanding about things they want and when they want it. Claude and Grace knew this first-hand as they watched the twins, Jacob and Joshua, and daughter, DJ, grow up. But for some reason, it was worse with the youngest two, Taylor and Stacey. Both of them had bad attitudes and wanted their way so much; it was perplexing and a problem. Claude and Grace had provided the best that they could. Yes, they struggled, but the kids had what they needed. Taylor and Stacey believed that since they were the youngest, did well in school, went to church, and merely existed, their parents should buy them whatever they wanted. The girls did not like being told "no," but they learned to tolerate it until one day, Stacey decided she and her sister should have special dresses for the school dance. Grace agreed that the dresses were gorgeous, but explained, again, that they could not afford the dresses. She was sure the girls had something in their closet, or they could go to the local thrift store or maybe catch a good sale at the department store. Unfortunately, Stacey did not accept what her mother said. Grace had left her wallet on the counter and Stacey copied the numbers from her credit card and ordered the dresses. Maybe if her mother had told her that they were behind on their mortgage and a few other bills were behind, just maybe she would have stopped herself since common sense didn't stop her. Stacey's impulsive and selfish behavior would bring additional troubles to the family by…

____

____

____

Complete the story above and list three ways you would handle this situation:

1.____

2.____

3.____

I. UNCOVERING THE CHAINS

Our session today is about dealing with our attitudes. The goal of this session is to explore how our attitude affects our decisions and to clarify the difference between things I want and things I need.

Memory Verse: *"And my God will meet all your needs according to his glorious riches in Christ Jesus"* (Philippians 4:19, NIV).

Reflect and share with someone why you think Paul said this. Are his words true in your life today and how?

____

____

A FINANCIAL STRONGHOLD MESSAGE FROM DR. SOARIES:

Read Luke 15:11-32. Here, Jesus tells one of his most famous parables. We call it the Parable of the Prodigal Son. This is a story about a young man who demanded his inheritance from his father before his father died. There are three things that are important to know about this young man:

1. He was impatient and could not wait until his father died to get his inheritance.

2. When he got his inheritance, he took all of his money with him to a distant location.

3. When he got to his destination, he spent all of his money on extravagant living.

When he had to get a menial job, his life was miserable. After he hit rock bottom, he decided to go back to his father to ask for help. Fortunately, his father welcomed him home with open arms. This story has a wonderful ending that shows a parent's unconditional love for his child and God's unconditional love for us. However, this story also teaches us a lesson about our finances. The son's problem was he mismanaged all of the money he had been in such a hurry to get.

I used to live just like this young man. I did not inherit a lot of money, but I did spend all of the money I earned as soon as I got paid. I used to tell my dad "I don't know where my money goes" as if my money left my house after I went to sleep at night! I thought the solution was to make more money. But having more money would have simply meant I would spend more money. I had to change my attitude about money and how to use it. Once I did that, I began to live differ- ently so I could have a productive life. My recovery started by determining the difference between things I wanted and things I needed.

Notice that when the father described the condition of his son, he used the word "dead." He had not died physically. However, his wasteful extravagance, his inability to defer gratification, and his lack of prudence in handling his affairs was a form of death. Likewise, when I possessed the same characteristics as this young man, I, too, was dead. That is why it takes more than informa- tion to get us on our financial feet. What it actually takes is a resurrection from the dead- and only God has the power to do that.

Barriers or Obstacles: I have discovered that I have the following problems due to impatience:

1.____

2.____

3.____

Scripture and Practical Living:

"The LORD is my shepherd, I lack nothing" (Psalm 23:1, NIV)

Share how this Scripture is a light to support you as you work through your barriers or ob- stacles.

____

____

II. BEGINNING TO BREAK AND ELIMINATE THE FINANCIAL CHAINS

Review Key Term(s):

Patience – "the ability to wait, or to continue doing something despite difficulties, or to suffer without complaining or becoming annoyed: (dictionary.cambridge.org)

Needs – "The things you must have for a satisfactory life" (dictionary.cambridge.org) .

Wants – "to feel a need or desire for: wish for"" (dictionary.com).

SUGGESTION BOX **Highlight the Key Term(s) or create an activity using the Key Terms**

Information and Statistics:

Statistics:

- Americans had a total of 1.5 billion credit cards. Fourteen percent of the population has more than 10 credit cards (creditcard.com).

- The average person seeking financial counseling is $43,000 in debt (Economy Watch).

Activity and Exercises

Grace was already frustrated as well as everyone else about the family's financial struggles. When children are involved, especially teens and preteens, what is their responsibility in helping with or making changes to the family financial problems—or are there responsibilities?

Let's do some investigating and see if we can find out what might be the cause of the family's problems and provide them with some solutions to help them. In helping them, we may even help ourselves or someone else we know. Reread their story and answer the following questions. You can do this individually or in groups:

- List possible reasons why Stacey thought she should have what she wanted:

1.____

2.____

3.____

- Write two consequences for Stacey because of her actions:

1.____

2.____

3.____

- Create two financial goals for Stacey and her parents:

1.____

2.____

Share your answers with the class. If you are working through the process by yourself, discuss with someone who is part of the **dfree®** ministry whom you trust or ask a close friend to review your response.

As I analyzed Claude and Grace's financial problems, I realized that I can provide help for others, and apply this to myself. Maybe Claude, Grace, and I, (________ first name) can benefit from some positive changes in my actions, thoughts, and feelings. Therefore, I will repeat the dfree® Affirmation statements of encouragement to myself. (Look in the mirror and repeat the dfree® Affirmation statements.)

dfree® Affirmation	1. I can change the way I think about my wants and needs. 2. There is power in waiting for what I want. 3. It is not too late for me to get started improving my financial status.

III. VICTORY STORY

"I am grateful for **dfree®** because it helped me to be more aware of my spending habits. I realized I was buying items I didn't need. I learned to stay focused on eliminating debt, and not to acquire new debt. Now I have a realistic plan for retirement."

– Donna

IV. COMMITMENTS AND ASSIGNMENT(S)

Review and complete the following assignments before you begin the next session.

Commitments: As a result of my discovery, I commit to the following actions:

1.____

2.____

3.____

Commitments: As a result of my discovery because of my impatience, I commit to the following actions:

Commitment #1: I will list at least ten personal needs and wants in the table below:

NEEDS	WANTS
1.	1.
2.	2.
3.	3.
4.	4.
5.	5.
6.	6.
7.	7.
8.	8.
9.	9.
10.	10.

Commitment #2: I will analyze my list of wants and needs and make sure each item is in the correct category.

Commitment #3: I will estimate the annual cost of my needs and write the amount next to each item.

Commitment #4: I will estimate the annual cost of my wants and write the amount next to each item.

Commitment #5: I will circle the items on my needs list that can wait.

Commitment #6: I will memorize the **dfree®** pledge:

I pledge to:

- ☐ *Apply biblical principles in managing my money*
- ☐ *Keep my expenses below my income*
- ☐ *Pay my bills on time*
- ☐ *Invest in assets that grow in value*
- ☐ *Contribute to my church and its ministries*

Commitment #7: I will attend the next **dfree®** session on _______ at _______ .

Benefits: As a result of keeping my commitments, my life will be better in the following ways:

1.______________________________

2.______________________________

3.______________________________

V. HOME ASSIGNMENTS: Read chapter four, "Start the Plan," in the dfree® book.

Answer the following after you have had a moment to reflect on the class, your situation, and to pray. Responsible Actions I need to schedule and do and say this week:

____

____

____

____

Closing prayer: *"Dear God, thank You for providing so many of my needs without me even ask- ing. Please give me the help I need to remember the difference between what I want and what I need and the patience to wait for both. Amen."*

Resources:

Kiplinger.com

Consumerjungle.org

Financiallit.org

Mint.intuit.com

dfree® Lifestyle

LEVEL TWO – GET CONTROL
STEP FOUR – START THE PLAN

Opening prayer: *"Dear God, I believe You can provide all my needs. I now need You to enable me to take control of my financial affairs and begin living the way You want me to live. Amen."*

Response: I will never arrive at my destination if I never begin my journey. "A journey of a thou- sand miles begins with one step."

LIFE SITUATION – READ AND ANSWER THE QUESTION(S) BELOW: Claude's Story – Injured in a Fire

Prayer is very important and our actions are too! As Christians, we should always make the time to pray and give thanks to God. But, Christians have moments in our lives when prayer doesn't seem to be working. We are so paralyzed or distraught by our emotions and our situation that we will not do anything. We get stuck.

It was a beautiful, sky-blue kind of day. The sun was showing off its brilliant, bright yellow and the clouds were lightly scattered across the soft blue. How could such a calm and serene day be- come so violent? Over the last few weeks, the weather forecasters were predicting a major storm, like Sandy, but no one believed them because it had not happened. Although nature was regal and crowned in glory, Claude was feeling cold and dejected. Three days ago, the storm did hit. Claude was at work when the storm came quickly and voraciously. As the storm raged, people ran for cover. For 20 minutes the storm raged and then another catastrophe began on the hills of the storm. As people tried to move and run out of the buildings, a fire was now raging throughout the business complex.

The fire occurred because a gas line had erupted from one of the nearby buildings. Claude was one of the people injured. He had gone back inside the building to rescue others. He found three people who were either unconscious or coughing profusely because of the smoke. Claude was able to take them out of the building. As he turned to try one more time, Claude collapsed and woke up in Community Hospital. The doctors said he would recover and probably needed to stay in the hospital at least another week, then recuperate at home for about another month or two. Although he had medical insurance, he had opted not to take short-term or long-term dis- ability because of the extra costs. As he gathered his thoughts, he could only ask, "Lord, what am I going to do?" If his wife's hours had not been cut for the next six months, he would not feel so overwhelmed. The credit card debt, family expenses, house repairs, and so much more were draining and weighing on him.

In addition to prayer, what suggestions or advice can you give Claude? By the way, they've al- ready spent half of their emergency savings because of an emergency last month, and their sav- ings have dwindled to $1,000 because of a bad investment.

I. UNCOVERING THE CHAINS

Our session today is about starting a plan. The goal of this session is to create and launch a new plan for using money.

Memory Verse: "Do not love the world or anything in the world" (from 1 John 2:15, NIV).

Reflect and share with someone why 1 John 2:15 was shared in ancient Biblical times. Are these words true in your life today and how?

___

___

A Financial Stronghold Message From Dr. Soaries:

Both of my grandmothers always had money. My father's mother was a seamstress with only a sixth grade education. Her husband suffered a stroke and was confined to a wheelchair after she had her sixth child. Although she faced extreme hardships — racial discrimination and financial limitations — when she died at 80 years of age, she owned three houses, all of which were completely free of mortgage debt.

My mother's mother was a domestic worker-she did housework for wealthy families. Her hus- band was an alcoholic and did not work. She raised eight children almost as a single parent. But she too owned her own house. Whenever one of my cousins or I needed money, my grandmother always had cash to assist us. There were no ATM machines in those days. If we asked Grandma for a few dollars, she would unbutton the top of her dress, dig into her bosom, and from a white handkerchief she kept in her bra, she would pull out two or three dollar bills and hand them to one of us. If we needed $15 or $20, Grandma would turn around, lift her dress, and pull some cash out of the top of her stocking. This was where she kept the large bills!

As I got older, it was amazing to me that both of my grandmothers did so much with such little income. They really knew how to handle money. What later became clear to me was neither one of my grandmothers felt the need to buy new clothes every time the style changed; they did not buy things at the supermarket that they did not need; and neither of them had credit cards. They both gave money to the church regularly and they owned their own homes.

I decided that if my grandmothers could accomplish what they did with the challenges they faced, and then shame on me if I could not do at least as well as they did. They were like the folks in Matthew 25:14-28 who received money from their master before he went on a journey. The owner gave one servant five talents (more than $5,000), a second two talents (more than $2,000) and a third servant one talent (more than $1,000). When the master returned from his trip, the first two servants had doubled the original amount they were given. The third servant, however, handed the master the exact same amount he had been given. This third man was chastised by the master because he did not even think to put the money in a bank to earn interest. Jesus said the master called the servant "worthless."

Barriers or Obstacles: I have discovered that I have some changes to make concerning what I do with money:

1.____

2.____

3.____

Scripture and Practical Living:

Reread Matthew 25:14-28 and share what skills or attitudes did the servants who made a profit possess that maybe the one who Jesus called "worthless" did not.

____

____

Share how this Scripture is a support to you as you work through your barriers or obstacles.

____

____

II. BEGINNING TO BREAK AND ELIMINATE THE FINANCIAL CHAINS

Review Key Term(s):

Spending leaks – those areas where expenses are taken from the budget without being noticed or adding value.

Cash flow – It is the net cash and cash equivalents transferred in and out of a company (investopedia.com/terms/c/cashflow)

Accountability – The acceptance of responsibility for honest and ethical conduct towards others (investopedia.com/terms/a/accountability.asp)

Support - To agree with and give encouragement to someone or something because you want him, her or it to succeed (dictionary.cambridge.org/dictionary/english/support).

Information and Statistics:

Statistics:

- 40% of American households spend more than they earn (Federal Reserve Bank).
- 57% of American households do not have a budget (Harris Interactive).
- 61% of American households live paycheck to paycheck (CareerBuilder).

Activity and Exercises

A big storm is coming in 30 days. Only persons completing this activity know it's going to hap- pen. The storm is predicted to destroy our entire town.

SUGGESTION BOX **Highlight the Key Term(s) or create an activity using the Key Terms**

1. What should happen in light of this news?

____

____

2. What are some of the barriers to executing the plan of action?

____

____

Share your answers with the class. If you are working through the process by yourself, discuss with someone who is part of the **dfree®** ministry whom you trust or ask a close friend to review your response.

As I analyzed Claude and Grace's financial problems, I realized that I can provide help for others, and apply this to myself. Maybe Claude, Grace, and I, (________ first name) can benefit from some positive changes in my actions, thoughts, and feelings. Therefore, I will repeat the dfree® Affirmation statements of encouragement to myself. (Look in the mirror and repeat the dfree® Affirmation statements.)

dfree® Affirmation

1. My goals are more likely to be achieved when they are written down.
2. There is someone in my life I can trust to help me reach my goals.
3. There are some things I want that I am determined to achieve.

III. VICTORY STORY

"My husband is a very proficient saver, and I'm a very proficient spender. I wanted to be better with my finances and be on the same page with him. A lot of the lessons I learned about saving have helped us to move forward to purchase a new home and we're very excited about that."

- Debra

IV. COMMITMENTS AND ASSIGNMENT(S)

Review and complete the following assignments before you begin the next session.

Commitments: As a result of my discovery that I need to make some changes, I commit to the following actions:

Commitment #1: I will list my short-term financial goals—things I would like to achieve within the next 12 months. Example: Create an emergency savings fund—Goal: At least $3,000.

1.____

2.____

3.____

4.____

5.____

Commitment #2: I will locate my spending leaks using the exercise below:

Spending Leaks

Many people think they cannot afford to cut anything from their regular expenses. Yet upon close analysis, people discover they have "spending leaks," or expenses that zap money from their budgets without them noticing or without adding value to their lives. They are often incidental items that seem small at the moment, but can add-up over time.

Potential Spending Leaks

A. ITEM	B. COST OF ITEM	C. ITEMS PURCHASED PER MONTH	D. COST PER MONTH (BXC)	E. COST PER YEAR (DX12)
Example: Coffee out	*$1.75*	*16*	*$1.75x16=$28*	*$28x12=$336*
Eating dinner out				

Take-out				
Premium cable TV package				
Movies				
Parking tickets				
Show tickets				
Magazine subscriptions				
Drinks/ night out with friends				
Buying lunch at work				
Lottery tickets				
Bank fees				
Coffee out				
Late fees on bills				
Impulse buys at grocery store				
Gifts				
Cell phone plan				
New clothes				
Bottled water				
Other				
Other				
Other				

If I weren't spending my money on ______________________________, I could use the ex- tra money to help accomplish the following short-term or long-term goals (if renting, consider making home ownership a goal; see www.hud.gov):

1.____

2.____

3.____

cash flow bottom line right now?

	CURRENT
Total Monthly Income	
Expenses	
Basics	
Housing (rent, mortgage)	
Property insurance	
Home maintenance	
Groceries	

	CURRENT
Health	
Medical/dental	
Prescriptions	
Vision/contacts	
Health insurance	
Doctor co-pays	
Life insurance	
Disability insurance	

Work/school lunches	
Cleaning supplies	
Grooming supplies (toiletries, hair, nails)	
Child care	
Child support/alimony	
Clothing	
Dry cleaning/laundry	
Tuition/school-related fees	
Other	
Utilities	
Electric/gas/oil	
Water/sewer	
Garbage	
Home phone	
Cell phone (all features)	
Internet	
Cable	
Other	
Transportation	
Car loan/lease	
Car insurance	
Gas/maintenance	
Parking	
Registration/inspection	
Public transportation	
Other	
Other	
Consumer Debt	
Credit cards (minimum payments)	
Loan repayments	
Medical bills	
Past due bills	
Other	
Personal	
Leisure/entertainment (movies, activities, eating out)	
Hobbies	
Travel/vacation	
Gifts	
Pets	
Spending money	
Charitable donations	
Other	
Savings	
Emergency savings	
Savings for financial goals	
Other	
TOTAL MONTHLY EXPENSES	

INCOME VS. EXPENSES	MONTHLY	ANNUAL
Total Income		
Total Expenses		
Cash Flow Surplus or Shortfall		

To start including savings for my financial goal into my spending plan, there are only three options:

1. Cut back on spending

2. Increase income

3. Do both

Circle the options that make the most sense for your current situation.

Commitment #5: I will revise my spending plan to better reflect my needs and wants.

Commitment #6: I will not try this alone.

Support is getting the resources and encouragement to help you reach your financial goals.

Accountability is having regular check-ins to monitor your progress, boost motivation, and reinforce your commitment to your goals.

I will ask three friends, family members, or **dfree®** participants to support me:

1.____

2.____

3.____

Three resources (books, blogs, websites, media) I will use for additional support:

1.____

2.____

3.____

How do I want to be held accountable for reaching my goals?

1.____

2.____

3.____

Commitment #7: I will attend the next **dfree®** session on ________ at ________ .

Benefits: As a result of keeping my commitments, my life will be better in the following ways:

1.____

2.____

3.____

- Identity Protection

Ten Things You Can Do in Ten Minutes or Less

Much like saving is about finding spending leaks, protecting your identity is about finding information leaks. The more information out there about you, the easier it is to be taken advantage of.

Information Leaks

1. Opt-out from prescreened credit card orders: www.optoutprescreen.com
2. Opt-out from most junk mail: www.dmachoice.org
3. Stop your paper bank statements and switch to email statements (if you have online banking).
4. Put a password-lock on your computer and phone.
5. Go through your email inbox and unregister or unsubscribe from mass email lists.

Setting up Safeguards

6. Arrange to receive texts or emails when your bank account has transactions above a certain limit.
7. Take your social security card out of your wallet.
8. Sign or put "SEE ID" on the back of your credit or debit card.
9. Photocopy everything you have in your wallet.
10. Pull your credit report at least once a year and check for any unusual activity.

V. HOME ASSIGNMENTS: Read chapter five, "Steer the Power" in the **dfree®** book.

Answer the following after you have had a moment to reflect on the class, your situation, and to pray. Responsible Actions I need to schedule and do and say this week:

____

____

Closing prayer: "Thank You, God, for opening my eyes and getting me started on a new path. Amen."

Resources:

	Mymoney.com	Hud.gov
	Mint.intuit.com	Empower.com
Youneedabudget.com	practicalmoneyskills.com	

dfree® Lifestyle

LEVEL TWO – GET CONTROL

STEP FIVE – STEER THE POWER

Opening prayer: *"God, help me to finish what I have started. Amen."*

Response: If I use the power I have, I can reach the goals I have set for my future.

LIFE SITUATION – READ AND ANSWER THE QUESTION(S) BELOW: Grace's Story — Get It Together

What is the use of knowing what to do or at least knowing where the resources are to help your- self, but you never try to make things happen? It is not a wise decision to wait on God to do for you when God has given you what you need to do the task or choose a fruitful option. We all can use assistance to help us when we are struggling or need a listening heart. There are many community resources available to help us, whether we struggle from addictions that may include drug/alcohol abuse to gambling to shopping (including shoes) to food (too much or too little).

Or maybe you just feel out of control or overwhelmed by life. Grace knew this all too well. She worked hard, loved her family and friends, helped others, and loved the Lord. Although she was active in church and prayed, the family's financial situation was too much to think about or handle at this time. Yet, she had to. Claude was recuperating from his injuries in the fire and she was left to handle most of the bills and issues of the house. Her parents and Claude's parents secretly helped out financially. No one wanted Claude to feel worse than he did and they wanted the fam- ily to have as normal a life as possible. His injuries and unhappiness were a burden at times, but Grace knew she could make it through whatever Claude needed medically and emotionally. Yet, the financial pains made her cry at night when the house was quiet and she did not know how she would make it through the night—let alone the next day. Grace wanted to make a plan, make a change, but where should she start?

Grace needed help that included a plan. In addition to prayer, what three things would you sug- gest she do to help bring the expenses under control?

1.____

2.____

3.____

I. UNCOVERING THE CHAINS

Our session today is about controlling your finances. The goal of this session is to take control of your financial future and use the new plan you created in chapter four.

Memory Verse: "I can do all things through Christ who strengthens me" (Philippians 4:13, NIV).

Reflect and share with someone why you think Paul said this. Are his words true in your life today and how?

____

____

A FINANCIAL STRONGHOLD MESSAGE FROM DR. SOARIES:

The Apostle Paul said this about himself: "When I was a child, I talked like a child, I thought like a child, I reasoned like a child. When I became a man, I put childish ways behind me" (1 Corinthians 13:11). Every Christian should be able to say this about some aspect of his or her life. And that includes money and finance. When I consider the way I used to think and live, not only must I admit I was "childish," but I often think I suffered from a form of mental deficiency. The truth is I was addicted to a lifestyle I had picked up from the culture. For instance, I really thought it was appropriate and acceptable to spend more money than I earned and to live above my means. What is so sad is that while I still thought and lived that way, I was actually leading other people both in the church and in the community.

When I first began serving as a minister, I decided I needed to look like a preacher. So instead of buying a small, used, affordable car, I drove Cadillacs and Lincoln Continentals. A car salesman stopped me one day when I was driving the Chevrolet that I could afford and told me it was wrong for me to be driving anything less than a Cadillac. And I believed him. He arranged for me to buy a Cadillac within two days. The payments took a big chunk, no, it took a huge chunk – out of my income every month.

When I bought the car, I checked out the radio and tape players and I learned about all the fancy gadgets. But I never asked what the interest rate was. But it did not matter. I looked good-and unfortunately, I felt good too! It would be years before I would realize it made better sense to own a small, used car than it did to drive a large, new car purchased with high interest rate financing.

After 15 years of living this way and experiencing the burden of debt, I broke free and started enjoying the benefits of debt-free living. It began when I did what you are doing and I started my "power strategy." That simply means I used as much patience as I could muster to make the largest payments I could afford to reduce my debt as quickly as possible. I called these my "power" payments-paying as much of the principal (actual balance due) as I could as often as I could.

Barriers or Obstacles: I have discovered that I can make the following changes:

1. I have discovered that I can do without ______________________________.
2. I have discovered that I can eliminate (a debt) ____________ by ____________ (date).
3. I have discovered that ____________________________ is really helping me to break free.

Scripture and Practical Living:

"Buy the truth and do not sell it; get wisdom, discipline and understanding" (Proverbs 23:23, NIV). Share how this Scripture is a support to you as you work through your barriers or obstacles.

____

____

II. BEGINNING TO BREAK AND ELIMINATE THE FINANCIAL CHAINS

Review Key Term(s):

Interest – It is the monetary charge for the privilege of borrowing money (investopedia.com/terms/i/interest.asp)

Principal – An amount of money that someone has invested in a bank or lent to a person or organization so that they will receive interest on it from the bank, person or organization (dictionary.cambridge.org/dictionary/english/principal)

SUGGESTION BOX **Highlight the Key Term(s) or create an activity using the Key Terms**

Information and Statistics

- A person can save $112,000 over a lifetime by bringing their lunch to work (saving.org).

Activity and Exercises

After reading Grace's story, with Claude's experience after the fire and both of their parents helping them, what things could Claude and Grade do to help each other feel empowered to control all areas of their lives?

____

____

Do you think Claude and Grace are committed to developing a plan and implementing it to control their lives? Explain your answer.

____

____

Share your answers with the class. If you are working through the process by yourself, discuss with someone who is part of the **dfree®** ministry whom you trust or ask a close friend to review your response.

As I analyzed Claude and Grace's financial problems, I realized that I can provide help for others and apply this to myself. Maybe Claude, Grace, and I, (________ first name) can benefit from some positive changes in my actions, thoughts, and feelings. Therefore, I will repeat the dfree® Affirmation statements of encouragement to myself. (Look in the mirror and repeat the dfree® Affirmation statements.)

dfree® Affirmation

1. I will have to sacrifice something to get ahead.
2. I must set my own priorities.
3. I believe that the future is now.

III. VICTORY STORY

"I am a 48-year-old single mother with an annual income of $52K. My accumulated debt resulted from not receiving child support and having to pay rent, daycare expenses, car note, food, clothes, and other day-to-day expenses. When I was able to buy my home, it required mainte- nance so I took out a second mortgage. My current relationship recently fell apart and all that we spent and planned on paying together is now mine to resolve.

When I first contacted people involved with **dfree®**, I was at the point where I could not sleep nor eat. My thoughts were on which creditor would be calling me tomorrow and how I would keep my promises to pay.

Since I took that first class, I learned what I was doing was wrong. I was paying on the creditors' schedule and not mine. I was paying their amounts and not what was suitable for me to maintain my household. I then contacted them with more authority in my way of speaking and with knowledge of my debts and income. Instead of speaking with the representative who answered, I requested to speak with someone with authority to make changes. I was able to change my payment due dates to meet my schedule. I then obtained a second job, working five evenings a week not far from my primary job. This is nice since I'm burning the same amount of gas traveling from home to and from work.

My credit card debt has now decreased from $35K to $28K, and my total debt, including my second mortgage, is below $100K. Although I am not in the clear, I have the confidence that I will break free from my debt."

- Anita

IV. COMMITMENTS AND ASSIGNMENT(S)

Review and complete the following assignments before you begin the next session.

Commitments: As a result of my discovery, I commit to the following actions:

Commitment #1: I will register for the free money management resource and tool at www.mint.intuit.com.

Commitment #2: I will complete the debt snowball and reduction activity below:

THE DEBT SNOWBALL PAYOFF METHOD

The basic steps in the debt snowball method are as follows:

1. List all debts in ascending order, from the smallest balance to the largest. This is the method's most distinctive feature: the order is determined by the amount owed, not the rate of interest charged. However, if two debts are very close in the amount owed, then the debt with the higher interest rate is moved toward the top of the list.
2. Commit to pay the minimum amount on every debt except the smallest.
3. Determine how much extra money can be applied toward the balance of the smallest debt.
4. Pay the smallest debt's minimum payment plus the extra money until the smallest debt is paid off. Note that some lenders (i.e., mortgage lenders, car companies) will apply extra amounts toward the next payment; in order for this payoff method to work, the lenders need to be contacted and told that the extra payments are to go directly toward principal reduction. Credit card companies usually apply the whole payment to the current cycle.
5. Once a debt is paid in full, add the old minimum payment (plus any extra amount available) from the first debt to the minimum payment on the second-smallest debt, and apply the new sum toward repaying the second-smallest debt.
6. Repeat until all debts are paid in-full.

Debt Snowball and Reduction Worksheet

Actively Working Toward Paying Off

DEBT	TOTAL PAYOFF	MINIMUM PAYMENT	EXTRA PAYMENT MONTHLY	PAYMENTS REMAINING	PLANNED CELEBRATION ACTIVITY
JCPenney	*$865*	*$35*	*$50*	*11*	*Cut up the card and never use it again!*

Next Debt to Pay Off

DEBT	TOTAL PAYOFF	MINIMUM PAYMENT	PAYOFF MOTIVATION	PAYMENTS REMAINING	PLANNED CELEBRATION ACTIVITY
Sears	*$2,100*	*$45*	*Extra money to put toward goal*	*23*	*One extra latte for the week!*

Remaining Debts

DEBT	TOTAL PAYOFF	MINIMUM PAYMENT	PAYOFF MOTIVATION	PAYMENTS REMAINING	PLANNED CELEBRATION ACTIVITY
Visa	*$3,568*	*$55*	*Increase credit score*	*65*	*Potluck dinner with family and friends*

Paid-Off Debts

DEBT	STARTING BALANCE	DATE PAID OFF	CELEBRATION ACTIVITY
Macy's	*$485*	*March 15, 2012*	*Had a clothing/accessory swap meet*

Commitment #3: I will calculate the cost I actually pay on my debts using the chart below:

CREDITOR	AMOUNT OWED	INTEREST RATE	ANNUAL INTEREST RATE PAID (AMOUNT X RATE)
1. EXAMPLE: VISA	*$2,000*	*17%*	*$2,000 x .17 (17%) = $340*
2.			
3.			
4.			
5.			
6.			
7.			
8.			
9.			
10.			
TOTAL			

Commitment #4: As I make payments on my debt, I will log them on the Billion Dollar Challenge (www.billiondollarpaydown.com) website.

Commitment #5: I will identify some things I can do to increase my income and use the increased income to make power payments on debt:

1.____________________

2.____________________

3.____________________

Commitment #6: I will reduce my spending in these areas:

1.____________________

2.____________________

3.____________________

Commitment #7: I will attend the next **dfree®** session on ________ at ________ .

Benefits: As a result of keeping my commitments, my life will be better in the following ways:

1.______________________________

2.______________________________

3.______________________________

V. HOME ASSIGNMENTS: Read chapter six, "Set the Timer" in the **dfree®** book.

Answer the following after you have had a moment to reflect on the class, your situation, and pray. Responsible Actions I need to schedule and do this week:

____

____

Closing prayer: *"God, in Your Word, You challenged me to be prepared. I am asking You to give me a humble spirit that can guide me to accept the changes I need to make to be prepared. Amen."*

Resources:

Powerpay.org

dfree® Lifestyle

LEVEL TWO – GET CONTROL

STEP SIX – SET THE TIMER

Opening prayer: *"Dear God, You gave us the gift of time. Help me use time in a meaningful way by assigning deadlines to my goals. Amen."*

Response: Understanding the relationship between time and money is crucial if I am to break free from debt and experience financial freedom.

LIFE SITUATION – READ AND ANSWER THE QUESTION(S) BELOW: The Clock Starts Now

Claude and Grace first had to stop avoiding the financial trouble they were in. They had gone to counseling sessions with Pastor Knight. This did allow them an opportunity to see how they could work together on their problems, keep their romance and marriage flavorful, and communicate better with the children. The sessions also offered practical ways to handle their ever-rising mountain of large and daunting debt. Pastor Knight gave them some financial resources to contact and they even wrote down steps to help them achieve their financial goals. Yet, they could not move—time was not on their side nor was the interest rates or the collectors that called.

Finally, the mortgage company called to say the house was in "pre-foreclosure," so Claude and Grace decided to take action and start putting their plan in motion.

Have you established a plan that will help you get out of debt or have you put a plan in motion? If yes, share what jump-started you?

____

____

I. UNCOVERING THE CHAINS

Our session today is about setting a schedule to accomplish your goal. The goal of this session is to actually make a timetable for your financial goals.

Memory Verse: "Teach us to number our days, that we may gain a heart of wisdom" (Psalm 90:12, NIV).

Reflect and share with someone why you think the Psalmist said this. Are these words true in your life today and how?

____

____

A FINANCIAL STRONGHOLD MESSAGE FROM DR. SOARIES:

I have been honored to visit the campus of Shaw University in Raleigh, North Carolina, every year for many years. When I visit Shaw, I always speak in the university's chapel. This is what the university's website says about its chapel:

> *"The History of the Thomas J. Boyd Chapel"*
>
> *The Thomas J. Boyd Chapel at Shaw University was first dedicated on June 15, 1948. The Chapel was completely renovated and rededicated on November 21, 1993. The renovation was made possible because of funds donated by Dr. Thomas J. Boyd, a 1948 Shaw graduate for whom the chapel was subsequently named.*
>
> *Two years after Shaw University was founded in 1865 by Dr. Henry Martin Tupper, the GBSC diligently raised funds to assist with the school's operations. Since then, the GBSC has continued its philanthropic support of Shaw, through scholarships and donations.*

What the website does not describe is how Rev. Boyd was able to donate $500,000 to his alma mater for the renovation of this beautiful chapel. He served as pastor of a Baptist church in Brooklyn, New York, for many years. Rev. Boyd told me that every time he performed a wedding, presided at a funeral, or did some other special service he would receive a gift from the parishioner. When he received these gifts, Rev. Boyd put them into a special account which became an investment account that grew over the years. As the fund grew, Rev. Boyd realized he had accumulated a substantial amount of money. He felt that he owed most of his success to what he learned as a student at Shaw University. As a result, he gave the school $500,000 to ensure that religious life at Shaw would always be housed in a nice facility. Recently, Rev. Boyd added an endowed lecture series, named after his wife, to his previous gift, to occur in the Boyd Chapel every year. I was honored to give the inaugural lectures of that endowed series.

Rev. Boyd says he never had a large salary, but he invested all of his extra income and allowed time for it to grow into a great sum of money. Now his legacy will live as long as there is a Shaw University.

Barriers or Obstacles: I have discovered I can take practical steps to make a difference in my life:

1. I have discovered I can save ____________________ by ____________________.

2. I have discovered that time affects the ______________________________ of money.

3. I have discovered it is possible to ______________________________ .

Scripture and Practical Living:

Rev. Boyd has lived his life embracing the wisdom of Proverbs 13:22a: "A good person leaves an inheritance for their children's children (NIV)."

Share how this Scripture is a support to you as you work through your barriers or obstacles.

____

____

II. BEGINNING TO BREAK AND ELIMINATE THE FINANCIAL CHAINS

Review Key Term(s):

Compound Interest – "interest on savings calculated on both the initial principal and the accumulated interest from previous periods (investopedia.com/terms/c/compoundinterest.asp)

Retirement – "The time of life when one chooses to permanently leave the workforce behind. (investopedia.com/terms/r/retirement.asp)

Information and Statistics:

SUGGESTION BOX **Highlight the Key Term(s) or create an activity using the Key Terms**

- 56% of Americans have less than $25,000 in savings or retirement (money.cnn.com)
- 51% of the workforce has no private pension coverage (www.ssa.gov).
- 34% of the workforce has no savings set aside specifically for retirement (www.ssa.gov).

Activity and Exercises

Compare what Claude and Grace have experienced with a situation in your life. Are there any simi- larities or differences? If yes, briefly explain.

____

____

Who or what did you turn to? ______________________________

What were the consequences of your crisis and depending on someone else to bail you out?

____

____

Did you make any promises that you have or have not kept from that situation?

____

____

Share your answers with the class. If you are working through the process by yourself, discuss with someone who is part of the **dfree®** ministry whom you trust or ask a close friend to review your response.

As I analyzed Claude and Grace's financial problems, I realized that I can provide help for others, and apply this to myself. Maybe Claude, Grace, and I, (________ first name) can benefit from some positive changes in my actions, thoughts, and feelings. Therefore, I will repeat the dfree® Affirmation statements of encouragement to myself. (Look in the mirror and repeat the dfree® Affirmation statements.)

dfree® Affirmation	
	1. A goal without a deadline is just a dream.
	2. Time is the most valuable asset I have.
	3. I can accomplish more than I ever imagined if I use the right system.

III. VICTORY STORY

"We're grateful for **dfree®** because it helped us to be on one accord as a couple. It took us beyond lip- service to action with a specific financial strategy. For example, with the snowball strategy, we decided which credit cards to pay and when. When we needed another car, we agreed that a used car would be better for us that we could buy outright, rather a new one that we had to finance. Now we have one vision, one strategy, one goal."

Arthur

IV. COMMITMENTS AND ASSIGNMENT(S)

Review and complete the following assignments before you begin the next session.

Time and Money Exercise

The earlier you can start saving, the more time you'll have to take advantage of the power of compounding interest.

The following chart illustrates monetary accumulation for two types of savers who want to retire by age 65.

RED started saving $1,200.00 per year into a tax-deferred account (no taxes paid on interest) that paid 12% per year (compounded yearly) at the age of 18, for only 10 years.

BLUE started saving $1,200.00 per year into a tax-deferred account that paid 12% per year (compounded yearly) but started at the age of 28, for 37 years (until he reached 65).

RED contributed a total of $12,000. **BLUE** contributed a total of $45,600.

WHO ACCUMULATED MORE MONEY?

AGE	DEPOSIT	ACCUMULATED BALANCE	AGE	DEPOSIT	ACCUMULATED BALANCE
18	$1,200.00	$1,200.00	18	$0.00	$0.00
19	$1,200.00	$2,544.00	19	$0.00	$0.00
20	$1,200.00	$4,049.28	20	$0.00	$0.00
21	$1,200.00	$5,735.19	21	$0.00	$0.00
22	$1,200.00	$7,623.42	22	$0.00	$0.00
23	$1,200.00	$9,738.23	23	$0.00	$0.00
24	$1,200.00	$12,106.81	24	$0.00	$0.00
25	$1,200.00	$14,759.63	25	$0.00	$0.00
26	$1,200.00	$17,730.79	26	$0.00	$0.00
27	$1,200.00	$21,058.48	27	$0.00	$0.00
28	$0.00	$23,585.50	28	$1,200.00	$1,200.00
29	$0.00	$26,415.76	29	$1,200.00	$2,544.00
30	$0.00	$29,585.65	30	$1,200.00	$4,049.28
35	$0.00	$52,140.03	35	$1,200.00	$14,759.63
40	$0.00	$91,888.54	40	$1,200.00	$33,634.93
45	$0.00	$161,939.01	45	$1,200.00	$66,899.66
50	$0.00	$285,391.86	50	$1,200.00	$125,523.47
55	$0.00	$502,957.97	55	$1,200.00	$228,838.66
60	$0.00	$886,383.80	60	$1,200.00	$410,915.33
65	$0.00	$1,562,111.12	65	$1,200.00	$731,796.64

RED accumulated $830,314.48 more than BLUE!

The earlier you can start saving, the more time you'll have to take advantage of the power of compounding interest. Even though **BLUE** put away almost four times more money than **RED**, **RED** had the advantage of time.

Commitments: As a result of my discovery, I commit to the following actions:

Commitment #1: I will make a list of my three-year goals and place dates next to each:

- Personal Goals
- Professional Goals
- Intellectual Goals
- Financial Goals

Commitment #2: I will calculate my retirement financial needs using the exercise below and create a plan for meeting them:

How much money will I need for retirement?

a. How long do I think I'll live? (age)	
b. At what age do I want to retire?	
c. How long do I estimate I'll spend in retirement? (a – b)	
d. What is my net monthly income now?	
e. What is my annual income? (d x 12 months)	
f. Any extra annual events/activities (activity x 3)	
g. Estimated retirement income needed (c x e + 6)	

Commitment #3: I will open or add to my investment account for long-term financial goals.

Commitment #4: I will review my spending plan to make sure it is accurate.

Commitment #5: I will sell the following assets/items and use the proceeds to pay off debts:

1.______________________________

2.______________________________

3.______________________________

4.______________________________

5.______________________________

6.______________________________

Commitment #6: I will read one article or book about personal finance.

Name of the book or article and author ______________________________

Commitment #7: I will attend the next **dfree®** session on __________ at __________.

Benefits: As a result of keeping my commitments, my life will be better in the following ways:

1.______________________________

2.______________________________

3.______________________________

V. HOME ASSIGNMENTS:

Read chapter seven, "Maximize the Margin" in the **dfree®** book. Answer the following after you have had a moment to reflect on the class, your situation, and pray. Responsible Actions I need to schedule and do this week:

Closing prayer: *"God, I believe this is the season for me to appreciate the value of time. Please bless the commitments I have made so I use the time You have given me to invest my resources wisely. Amen."*

Resource:

Ownthedollar.com

Annualcreditreport.com

Consumerfinance.gov/credit-cards

dfree® Lifestyle

LEVEL THREE – GET AHEAD

STEP SEVEN – MAXIMIZE THE MARGIN

Opening prayer: *"Dear God, I want to live the way You made me to live. Forgive me for the mis- takes I have made and help me live an entire life that pleases You. Amen."*

Response: I realize that if I want something I have never had, I must do something I have never done.

LIFE SITUATION – READ AND ANSWER THE QUESTION(S) BELOW: Moving Forward

As the children grew older, their expenses did too. Five children with five unique likes and desires, and cares that included braces, sporting events, cell phones, food, college tuition, clothes, activities, and the ever-growing "I need list." Joshua and Jacob were headed for college. Jacob had a full scholarship because of his academics, and Joshua's scholarship paid for his tuition, but not housing. Financially, this would have been fine for their parents 10 years ago, but life circumstances had changed that. Not only were the twins going to college, everyone else in the family had something that had a price tag.

Claude and Grace did not want to ask their parents again for help. Claude found out that his parents and his in-laws had helped while he was recuperating from his injuries in the fire. Although he was very grateful, he did not want to impose upon them anymore. He planned to pay them back as soon as possible.

In the meantime, Claude and Grace were revising their debt-free plan and making decisions about which of the children's needs or wants could be met. They even met with the twins' respective college financial aid officers to set up payment plans. The twins, Jacob and Joshua, and the girls, DJ, Taylor, and Stacey, were part of the financial planning process as well. Once they better understood what was really happening and the strain the family's finances put on their parents, each one could start to rethink their needs. Each child thought of ways they could financially contribute and started to reassess their spending habits. Jacob and Joshua played music at various social events and produced videos. Taylor wrote songs for the boys to sing. DJ and Stacey increased their babysitting time. The family worked together to make a difference. Hopefully, this will last!

List ways that you can talk with your children, family, or friends (if needed), about financial strategies that will increase your debt-free attitude and behavior.

1.____

2.____

3.____

I. UNCOVERING THE CHAINS

Our session today is about getting out of debt quicker and planning a better financial future.

The goal of this session is to address how to accelerate the process of getting out of debt and securing your financial future.

Memory Verse: "No temptation has overtaken you except what is common to humankind. And God is faithful; he will not let you be tempted beyond what you can bear. But when you are tempted, he will also provide a way out so that you can endure it" (1 Corinthians 10:13).

Reflect and share with someone why you think Paul said this. Are his words true in your life today and how?

____

____

A FINANCIAL STRONGHOLD MESSAGE FROM DR. SOARIES:

Jesus said so many things about money. The lessons He taught about using money were good for much more than just financial truths. In one sense, Jesus understood that the commitment to manage money was actually a commitment to manage our entire lives. But Jesus also said He had come so we could have the best quality of life (John 10:10). In Luke 16, Jesus tells the story of the shrewd manager who organized and executed a strategy to get out of financial trouble with his boss. I'm sure when that manager was in trouble, he felt like he'd hit rock bottom. But he got out - and we can get out, also.

When I was drowning in debt, I could not even imagine ever becoming debt-free—much less wealthy. But four years after I made the commitment to get out of debt, I was able to meet with a realtor about buying a home and tell her that my wife and I had no debt. She was shocked. She said she had never met anyone who had no debt at all.

It was a good thing that was true. We were able to qualify for a mortgage and close on the purchase of our new house within four weeks. We were able to get the lowest interest rate the bank offered. This was the first time I ever had debt that could be considered good debt. Although debt-free living strives to be free of ALL debt, borrowing at reasonable interest rates to purchase an asset that grows in value (like most real estate) can be considered "good" debt.

The way we got there was by taking small steps and making debt-free living our priority. The benefits were too many to mention but the key was to believe it was possible and believe that nothing else was more important.

That is what I respect about so many of my friends who have immigrated to America. They came here believing that America is indeed a land of opportunity, and they made it a priority to make good things happen for themselves and their families. They didn't mind sacrificing to attain their goals.

One young immigrant who bought prime real estate in my community made tremendous sacrifices to get where he was. By the time he was 24 years old; he had purchased prime urban property and owned the two businesses that were on that property. When I was 24 years old, I did not own anything and had no plans to own anything. I didn't even want to own a house because I did not feel like cutting grass. When I was a kid cutting the grass at our home, I promised myself that when I grew up, I would never cut grass. By owning nothing, I kept my promise to myself! I completely ignored the value of real estate, the significance of ownership, and the wealth that could accrue if I bought a house at age 24. I was "cool" but I was broke and had no assets.

Now that I live committed to a debt-free lifestyle, I still need encouragement and support to sustain the progress I have made. It is easy to start something, but it can be difficult to continue what we start. There are temptations all around us that seek to lure us back into the habits we have recently broken, but the same will power and support that helped us out of financial hardship can keep us out!

Barriers or Obstacles:

I have discovered that I can achieve financial freedom faster if I do three things:

1.____

2.____

3.____

Now, I plan to do them.

Scripture and Practical Living:

"Go to the ant, you sluggard; consider its ways and be wise!" (Proverbs 6:6, NIV).

Share how this Scripture is a support to you as you work through your barriers or obstacles.

____

____

II. BEGINNING TO BREAK AND ELIMINATE THE FINANCIAL CHAINS

Review Term(s):

Wealth - a large amount of money or possessions (britannica.com/dictionary/wealth)

Financial advisor – "A professional who provides expertise for clients' decisions around money matters, personal finances, and investments (investopedia.com/terms/f/financial-advisor.asp)

Financial planner – "A professional who works with clients to help them manage their money and reach their long-term financial goals (investopedia.com/terms/f/financialplannet.asp)
Insurance professional – "Adjusters, managing general agents, surplus line brokers" (lawinsider.com/dictionary/insurance-professional)

Tax advisor – Tax advisors are accounting professionals with advanced training and knowledge of tax accounting and law (carta.com/blog/tax-advisor)

SUGGESTION BOX **Highlight the Key Term(s) or create an activity using the Key Terms**

Information and Statistics:

- $117 billion worth of fast food is charged every year on credit cards (economywatch.com).
- 62% of Americans cannot cover unexpected expenses (cnbc.com).

Activity and Exercises

Claude and Grace's family "moving forward" story sounds too good to be true! Who talks their children in a meaningful way about finances? Not just discussions of an allowance or how much something costs, but conversations that incorporate financial terms, the economy, investments, and consequences that may happen if someone is not careful how they spend their money.

How often do you sit down with your family members to discuss the family's present and future financial picture?

- List possible reasons why you cannot or have not discussed your financial situation with your family (this does not mean to include all relatives, only those who live with you, those for whom you are responsible, or those to whom you financially contribute in some way):

1. ______________________________

2.____

3.____

- Create two financial goals for you and your family:

1.____

2.____

Share your answers with the class. If you are working through the process by yourself, discuss with someone who is part of the **dfree®** ministry whom you trust or ask a close friend to review your response.

As I analyzed Claude and Grace's financial problems, I realized that I can provide help for others, and apply this to myself. Maybe Claude, Grace, and I, (________ first name) can benefit from some positive changes in my actions, thoughts, and feelings. Therefore, I will repeat the dfree® Affirmation statements of encouragement to myself. (Look in the mirror and repeat the dfree® Affirmation statements.)

dfree® Affirmation

1. There is nothing wrong with attaining wealth.
2. Money can be used for some very good purposes.
3. Financial health is almost as important as physical health.

III. VICTORY STORY

"Several years ago, we bought into the concepts of **dfree®** and began implementing them into our lives. We were holding our own and didn't consider ourselves in financial hardship until we looked ahead and realized we hadn't really planned very far in advance for emergencies, or retirement, or anything. Upon recently finding out that both of our current jobs will end December 31st of this year, my wife and I are in a far better position financially to deal with an unforeseeable future as it relates to our careers.

The notion of being **dfree®**—no debt, no delinquencies, no deficiencies—is even more real when one's immediate future holds the prospect of being without a job. We haven't panicked and know that we will weather this season of our lives with the help of the **dfree®** principles we've learned and continue to practice."

- David and Carrie T.

IV. COMMITMENTS AND ASSIGNMENT(S)

Review and complete the following assignments before you begin the next session.

Commitments: As a result of my discovery, I commit to the following actions:

Commitment #1: I will identify financial professionals to advise me as I pursue my goals:

1. Insurance Professional: ______________________________
2. Financial Advisor/Planner: ______________________________
3. Tax Advisor: ______________________________

Commitment #2: I will track my spending again to make sure I am still on-track.

Commitment #3: Now that I have professional advisors, I will ask for help with the issue or is- sues that make me feel like I am stuck and will never reach my financial goals.

Commitment #4: The greatest obstacles I face in my financial journey are:

1.______________________________

2.______________________________

3.______________________________

Commitment #5: I will determine if I can lower debt payments by refinancing one or more items:

1.______________________________

2.______________________________

3.______________________________

Commitment #6: I will envision what I would do if I were wealthy. I would do the following with my money:

1.______________________________

2.______________________________

3.______________________________

Commitment #7: I will attend the next **dfree®** session on ________ at ________.

Benefits: As a result of keeping my commitments, my life will be better in the following ways:

1.______________________________

2.______________________________

3.____

V. HOME ASSIGNMENTS: Read chapter eight, "Minimize the Stress" in the **dfree®** book. Answer the following after you have had a moment to reflect on the class, your situation, and pray. Responsible Actions I need to schedule and do this week:

Closing prayer: *"God, the earth belongs to You and I am Your child. I want to be a blessing to my family and others who need my help. I intend to follow Your instructions and accept Your blessings in order to make a difference in someone else's life. Amen."*

Resources:

Ownthedollar.com
Federalreserve.gov/credit card
Ehow.com

Nonprofitrisk.org
Investorwords.com
Annualcreditreport.com

dfree® Lifestyle

LEVEL THREE – GET AHEAD

STEP EIGHT – MINIMIZE THE STRESS

Opening prayer: *"Dear God, You promised to care for each of us but You instructed us to place all of our cares on You and be anxious for nothing. Thank You for Your love and care. Direct my path to care for myself better and make decisions that minimize my own anxiety. Amen."*

Response: Whatever is worth having is worth protecting.

LIFE SITUATION – READ AND ANSWER THE QUESTION(S) BELOW: The Road to College

DJ knew for certain that her family had saved for her college education. The family had made changes to their spending and saving habits, so she figured they must have money saved for her to go to college. DJ was right. Her parents had saved, but the money had to be used for her brothers' college expenses and other household needs. DJ couldn't believe it! What would she do and where would she attend school? She was very upset with her parents and felt be- trayed. She talked with her friends, siblings, and grandparents about her feelings and thoughts. DJ prayed and cried. Eventually, she was calm enough to think about her alternatives and started putting ideas into action. Looking for scholarships and talking with the financial office of various schools became a full-time job for her. She spoke with her high school counselor and met with the various college representatives that visited the school. Although her parents could not afford the college tour bus trip the church offered, they did take her on a few local college visits. She invited two of her friends to come along and they all had a great time. One of her friends decided to apply to a school they'd visited.

How do you respond when you cannot buy nor have something you want because the financial costs are too great or you did not adequately plan for the expenses?

____

____

I. UNCOVERING THE CHAINS

Our session today is about minimizing the stress. The goal of this session is to financially prepare for the unexpected.

Memory Verse: "A good person leaves an inheritance for their children's children, but a sinner's wealth is stored up for the righteous" (Proverbs 13:22, NIV).

Reflect and share with someone why you think Solomon said this. Are his words true in your life today and how?

A FINANCIAL STRONGHOLD MESSAGE FROM DR. SOARIES:

Nothing is more important than to be prepared for the unexpected. In Matthew 25:1-13, Jesus describes what happened when ten young ladies traveled to a wedding but five of them had insufficient oil for use at the appropriate time. What the unprepared young ladies of the story did not know was that the bride- groom would be delayed. The moral of the story is that we should be prepared for our futures. In life, the unexpected should be considered likely to occur. And we must be prepared.

Dr. Martin Luther King, Jr. was assassinated when he was 39 years old. Just weeks before his death, Dr. King signed his life insurance documents, which he had been avoiding for years. As a result of his life insurance policy, his widow, Coretta Scott King, received a check every month from his insurer until the day the she died 38 years later.

We experience stress when circumstances in our lives change or when traumatic events occur. When we prepare properly for life's possibilities, we are better able to manage the stress that accompanies disruptive events.

One of my students and church members is 45 years old and has a condition that has prevented her from working for the past three years. However, because she had purchased extra disability insurance she has as much income as she did when she was working. She is stress free!

Smartmoney magazine has reported "the reality is one-third of all Americans between the ages 35 and 65 will become disabled for more than 90 days, according to the American Council of Life Insurers. One in seven workers will be disabled for more than five years. And while many people think that disabilities are typically caused by freak accidents, the majority of long-term absences are actually due to illnesses, such as cancer and heart disease. The loss of income can be so devastating that it forces some people into home foreclose or even bankruptcy."

One of my most painful professional encounters was having to tell four grown siblings that our church would not pay for their mother's funeral. They all had jobs, they all had gone on vacations, but none of them had any money to pay for the funeral and their mother had no insurance. I explained to them that our church would go out of business if we paid for every member's funeral. They were extremely upset; I thought they should have been extremely embarrassed.

When we fail to prepare for life's possibilities, we are vulnerable to stress and we are also gambling with our futures. Nothing exempts us from needing to be prepared.

Barriers or Obstacles: I have discovered that I am unprepared and vulnerable in the following areas:

1.____________________________________

2.____________________________________

3.____________________________________

4.____________________________________

Scripture and Practical Living:

"Commit to the LORD whatever you do, and your plans will succeed" (Proverbs 16:3, NIV, 1995, Zondervan)

Share how this Scripture is a support to you as you work through your barriers or obstacles.

____

____

II. BEGINNING TO BREAK AND ELIMINATE THE FINANCIAL CHAINS

Review Key Term(s):

Insurance - an arrangement by which a company gives customers financial protection against loss or harm such as theft or illness in return for payment premium (course.uceusa.com).

Will – "A legal document by which a person, the testator, expresses their wishes as to how their property is to be distributed at death and names one or more persons, the executor, to manage the estate until its final destination (comtois.hk/services/will)

Estate – "Everything you own; all of your assets (whether real property or personal property) and liabilities" (vocabulary.com/dictionary/estate)

Probate – "The act of proving that an instrument purporting to be a will was signed and executed in accord with legal requirements" (vocabulary.com/dictionary/probate)

SUGGESTION BOX **Highlight the Key Term(s) or create an activity using the Key Terms**

Information and Statistics:

- Medical problems contribute to 62% of all U.S. personal bankruptcies and home foreclosures each year (investopedia.com).
- In 2013, of the U.S. population with disabilities, over half (51.9%) were people ages 18-64. Forty percent (40.3%) of people with disabilities were 65 and older, while children and youth with disabilities accounted for only 7.4% (ages 5-17) and 0.4% (under 5 years old) (disabilitycompendium.org)
- Just over one in four of today's 20-year-olds will become disabled before reaching age 67. (ssa.gov)

Activity and Exercises

Knowing and understanding the various types of insurance is important to managing our finances.

ISSUES OF IMPORTANCE

After you read through the insurance information, you may decide to make an appointment with someone from the Human Resource Department on your job regarding short-term and long-term disability and other insurance plans that your employer may offer. Also, speak with an insurance professional who can share information regarding various types of insurance. There are many types of insurance options for the different stages and ages in our lives. Start learning more about your options now and for the future.

Leaving a positive legacy that encourages financial freedom should be applied to the administrative matters that others will have to take care of if unable to - such as funeral and burial needs, hospitalization, nursing home, military duty, and more. Do not feel discouraged because you cannot learn all the information at one time. Read and review the various sections more than once by yourself and with an insurance professional. The topics and exercises that are included for you to read will help you have a better understanding and control over your financial freedom.

Divide insurance information into groups to help you read through the information and reflect on how it applies to me today, how it can apply to me in the future and how I can share this information with someone else.

- **Disability Insurance**

Not able to work due to illness or non-work-related injury? Learn more about short-term and long- term disability. Highlight key words and phrases that will help you remember.

What is short-term and long-term disability insurance?

Short-term disability begins immediately after you are not able to work because of an illness or the birth of a child. Employers may have short-term disability, known as sick leave, non-work related injury, or may be identified by another name that may only include a small number of days, months, or a year. The length of time that you have been employed may be a factor as well. Short- term disability insurance may be offered also. Check with your Human Resource Department if you have any questions or need additional information. Check the state laws regarding short-term disability. Some states are required to have short-term disability, but not long-term disability.

Long-term disability insurance replaces a pre-determined portion of an employee's income if a qualifying disability involving a non-occupational injury or illness lasts at least three to six months- depending on the policy. Some employers provide employees with a basic level of group cover- age, typically paying an insured worker approximately 60% of his or her salary when they encounter a qualifying long-term disability. These benefits packages may also offer employees the option to purchase supplementary coverage.

Know what your employer provides

Determine if your employer provides short-term and/or long-term disability coverage. If so, find out the basics of the contract:

- What percentage of your income would the coverage replace in the case of short-term and long-term disability?
- When would you start receiving the benefit after experiencing a disability? After three months? After six months?
- Whether you would qualify for disability benefits only if you can't perform your current job, or if you can't perform any job at all.

Purchasing Group Disability Insurance

Though some employers provide long-term disability insurance to full-time employees, others offer group voluntary coverage, which provides employees the option to purchase group long- term disability insurance at their own expense. Though workers pay the full cost, voluntary group insurance allows workers to:

- Pay group insurance premium rates, which are often more favorable than individual insurance rates.
- More easily obtain coverage at a competitive premium rate, since buying individual insurance often requires underwriting tests and more stringent qualification limitations.

HOMEOWNERS/RENTERS/CONDOS INSURANCE

Whether you are renting or buying, or own the dwelling that you live in, good coverage is important to have. Having your belongings protected against fire, theft, and other types of damage is important. Read the information provided below regarding the various types of insurance that is offered for where you live. Check with an insurance professional if you any questions and need additional information.

- **Homeowner's Insurance**

Mortgage lenders require insurance and owners should make sure they understand their policy and know what is covered and what is not covered.

- **Renters Insurance**

When renting a house, condo, or apartment, the landlord carries insurance only on the building. It's up to you to insure anything inside the unit by purchasing renters insurance.

- **Condo Insurance**

Sometimes a condo association's master insurance policy will provide dwelling coverage. Per- sonal property and personal liability, however, can only be covered under a personal condo insurance policy. It's important to remember that even if your condo association's master insurance policy covers your condo for fire and other similar situations, it still does not protect your personal property or provide personal liability. You will be taking a huge financial risk if you don't have condo insurance.

AUTO-VEHICLE INSURANCE

Protect your vehicle and yourself by having adequate insurance to protect any damages or vehicle related circumstances that may occur. Shop around to find the best coverage for your needs.

- **Auto Insurance**

A few factors need consideration in order to make an educated decision on auto insurance cover- age. First, what is the state-required minimum coverage where you live? Second, what does the minimum cover? Third, what other coverage is available and can you afford it? Fourth, what are you protecting?

- **Umbrella Insurance**

You should also consider umbrella options that offer extra coverage to fill any coverage gaps that may exist in the policy. Umbrella policies may also provide coverage for claims that may be excluded by the primary policy

- **Professional Liability Insurance**

Coverage for specialists in various professional fields is important information to know. Since basic liability policies do not protect against situations arising out of business or professional pursuits, professional liability insurance is purchased by individuals who hold themselves out to the general public as having greater than average expertise in particular areas. (Barons Insurance Dictionary) Federal government employees can be reimbursed for 50% of their cost for professional liability insurance.

FEDERAL WORKERS

If you are employed by the Federal Government and want or need professional insurance coverage, learn more about the Federal Employee Defense Services (FEDS). FEDS offers various types of "Professional Liability Insurance for the Federal Community," (governmentworkerfi.com/federal-employees-professional-liability-insurance/)). FEDS provides services that range from Legal to Supplemental Disability Insurance, webinars, headline news stories, family medical cost, flexible spending and more. The costs for the various services are provided on the website. Join FEDS and learn more about how the Federal Government can assist with professional liability insurance and other insurance needs or questions.

ESTATE PLANNING/FUNERAL AND FUNERAL PLANNING

Although the following topics may be difficult for you to read, process, and put in place, you are helping your loved ones and friends who will have the responsibility of honoring your request and handling the legal and plethora of business that must be attended to. Think of others now!

Take a moment to breath out, breath in, and now read the next topics... slowly.

- **Estate Planning – Will**

Estate planning is the process of anticipating and arranging for the disposal of an estate.

A will is a legal document that defines who will receive your assets, who the executor (the per- son in charge of handling the estate) will be, how the assets will be distributed, and numerous other issues. In short, having a will allows you to determine who will benefit from your estate and assets after your death.

Why you need one:

- You can determine who will benefit from your estate and assets after your death.
- Your spouse or children may not get what you intended for them to have without one.
- Your estate will be divided by the government if there is no will present.

- You can avoid probate difficulties

How to get started:

1. Draft a letter of instruction. This letter outlines specific requests you'd like carried out, such as funeral, burial, and cremation arrangements. It also lists meaningful possessions you'd like to give to specific loved ones and important contacts such as your employer or insurance agent. Overall, it helps to clarify your intentions and prepare the will.

2. Consider other important legal documents to include:
   - Living will—expresses medical treatments you want or refuse
   - Health care proxy/power of attorney—delegates someone to make health care decisions for you if you are unable to do so
   - Durable power of attorney—delegates someone to handle financial matters
   - Guardianship documents—address the needs and care of children under 18

3. Meet with an attorney to draw up and finalize the above documents. Contact the American Bar Association for a list of free or low-cost legal services in your state. Also check with your employer, union, or trade association. Ask colleagues, friends, and family for referrals.

4. After documents are completed:
   - Sit down with your family to discuss all matters
   - Keep documents in a safe, accessible place
   - Review all documents every few years

     – Make changes as your family situation changes (for example, the birth of children or grandchildren, or a divorce).

Discovery: I will complete the personal financial risk assessments below to uncover the areas where I am lacking protection.

Personal Risk Assessment

1. I am satisfied with my current financial strategy.	Yes	No
2. I know how much I will need to retire and how much I can safely withdraw from my assets in retirement.	Yes	No
3. I have a six-month to one-year cash emergency fund.	Yes	No
4. I have health insurance for my family and me.	Yes	No
5. I have adequate life insurance to provide for my family.	Yes	No
6. I have disability insurance.	Yes	No
7. I have personal liability insurance.	Yes	No

8. I have a will, power of attorney, living will, and healthcare proxy.	Yes	No
9. My beneficiary designations for my life insurance and retirement accounts match those in my estate plan or will.	Yes	No
10. I review my financial situation on an annual basis with a certified financial planner.	Yes	No

If I answered "No"

0-1 times = Low risk

2-3 times = Moderate risk

4 times or more = High risk

Discovery: I will complete the following exercise to determine how much personal insurance I need.

PERSONAL INSURANCE

- **Disability Insurance**

If I become sick or disabled, either temporarily or permanently, would I be able to support myself and my family? Yes ________ No ________

How much income would I need? ________________________________

Are there any additional needs I should consider? ________________________

What are my options to cover this need?

- Spouse/partner income
- Savings
- Disability Income from insurance or employer

  – What long-term disability insurance typically pays: slightly over half of current income (current income x 60%).

- **Life Insurance**

If I were to die suddenly, would there be dependents left without basic support? Yes ________ No ________

Would my burial costs impose undue hardship on others? Yes ________ No ________

How much life insurance do I need?

Burial costs: ___________

Ten times my annual salary:

D.I.M.E. method: Debt + Income + Mortgage + Education:

Discovery: I have discovered that I am unprepared and vulnerable in the following areas:

1.____

2.____

3.____

4.____

I can benefit from some positive changes in my actions, thoughts, and feelings. Therefore, I will repeat the **dfree®** Affirmation statements of encouragement to myself. (Look in the mirror and repeat the **dfree®** Affirmation statements.)

dfree® Affirmation	
	1. The unexpected will happen.
	2. It pays to be prepared.
	3. If we fail to plan, we plan to fail.

III. VICTORY STORY

"When I heard your message, I realized that I was not prepared for any illness that may happen to me. Being a small business owner if I had a major illness my business would be in jeopardy. I re- cently took steps to purchase disability insurance that will provide a set amount of monies to cover any expenses for my business and personal life for a period of two years. I want to thank you for delivering that timely message and I now feel at ease knowing that if anything happens, my business will survive until I get back on my feet."

- V.W.

IV. COMMITMENTS AND ASSIGNMENT(S)

Review and complete the following assignments before you begin the next session.

Commitments: As a result of my discovery, I commit to the following actions:

Commitment #1: I will calculate how much life insurance I need and set a date to establish the required coverage.

Commitment #2: I will consider my options for disability insurance and set a date to establish the coverage I need.

Commitment #3: I will make sure I have sufficient insurance coverage on my house or apartment.

Commitment #4: I will make sure I have sufficient health insurance for my entire family and will ask someone for suggestions about improving my coverage.

Commitment #5: I will set a date to complete my will and my healthcare directive (living will).

Commitment #6: I will designate a certified financial planner to meet with at least once a year.

Commitment #7: I will attend the next **dfree®** session on _______ at _______.

Benefits: As a result of keeping my commitments, my life will be better in the following ways:

1.______________________________

2.______________________________

3.______________________________

V. HOME ASSIGNMENTS: Read chapter nine, "Maintain the Focus" in the **dfree®** book.

Answer the following after you have had a moment to reflect on the class, your situation, and pray. Responsible Actions I need to schedule and do this week:

____

____

Closing prayer: *"Lord, teach me to number my days and to be prepared as I live and prepare for the end of my days. Amen."*

Resources:

estateplanning.com
agingwithdignity.org
insurancecalculators.com
disabilitycanhappen.org
insure.com

dfree® Lifestyle

LEVEL THREE – GET AHEAD

STEP NINE – MAINTAIN THE FOCUS

Opening prayer: *"Dear God, protect me from distractions that would take my eyes off You and Your will for my life. Amen."*

Response: I will keep my eyes on the prize.

LIFE SITUATION – READ AND ANSWER THE QUESTION(S) BELOW: Don't Be Fooled

Today was a special day for the family. They had planned a fun vacation for three days and two nights. The travel agent promised they would enjoy themselves and have a wonderful time. Well, everyone saved so they could have spending money and be able to eat a wonderful dinner to- gether at least once. The island looked like paradise, but when the family arrived at the hotel, things began to change. The hotel rooms were not clean and the lounge area was not the pret- tiest, but they thought they could tolerate it. Once the rooms were cleaned, they could unpack and head to the beach.

However, the warm, white sands shown in the virtual tour and in the brochure were not visible. Plus, they had paid an extra $700 for excursions and evening events. Grace thought they had wasted their money and Claude was planning to sue the travel company for false advertisement. The kids decided to spend as much time on the beach as possible and go souvenir shopping since the fun events scheduled were cancelled. The family was disappointed, but happy they were all together. As everyone settled in, Stacey created some games they could all play and searched online for local carnivals and street shows. Although they did not have all the amenities they wanted, they made the vacation work.

What advice can you give Claude and Grace on planning for future vacations or other events? Do you think they spent money that was not in their budget plan?

____

____

I. UNCOVERING THE CHAINS

Our session for today is to maintain focus. Therefore, the goal of this session is to take meaning- ful steps toward your financial goals.

Memory Verse: "No one can serve two masters. Either you will hate the one and love the other, or you will be devoted to the one and despise the other. You cannot serve both God and money" (Matthew 6:24, NIV).

Reflect and share with someone why you think the Gospel writer Matthew said this. Are his words true in your life today and how?

____

____

A FINANCIAL STRONGHOLD MESSAGE FROM DR. SOARIES:

I receive an invitation to borrow money almost every day. Many of them are quite tempting. They appeal to my ego. They appeal to my appetites. The letters credit card companies write are so im- pressive. They compliment me and make me feel important. Despite the fact that millions of other people have received the same letter, they make it sound as if I am the only person in the world receiving their message. And then there is the pre-qualification for the right to use their card and pay their high interest rates. Everything from special colors and logos to a "supposed" zero interest rate makes every letter somewhat appealing. I have learned that the best way to resist these orders is to not open the envelope at all.

Then there is the email offer to lend me $1,500 with no credit check—all within an hour. What they don't tell me is that I will have to pay the money back at an interest rate of 400-800% and I will probably end up in a debt trap that will take months and more loans to escape. It can be hard to avoid the traps that are set and designed to take our money.

Then there are the attractive store sales. A store near me sells three suits for the price of one a few times a year. When I was younger, I would buy the suits just because of the price. But I have grown up and I realize that unless I need a new suit, there is no price that makes sense to pay for a new suit.

Advertising and marketing strategies abound, and in this age of endless media, we are encouraged to part with our money all the time - 24/7. That makes it imperative for us to have a strategy to remain focused so we can stay faithful to our **dfree®** commitments.

That commitment includes increasing our incomes. No one wants to struggle and juggle for the rest of his or her life. One solution for dealing with increasingly higher costs of living is drawing a higher income. I know that sounds difficult or even impossible. But everyone does something well enough to get someone to pay them to do it. That is the key to earning more money. It starts by looking squarely at yourself - very carefully - and answering the question, "What do I do so well that some- one will pay me to do it?" Don't be humble about it - make a list of your most outstanding attributes and talents, and then figure out who will pay you how much to do it for them.

The other way to figure out a strategy for increasing income is to identify something you love to do - something you love so much that you would almost feel guilty taking money for doing it. Everyone has an answer to that question. Even shoppers!

Did you know that companies compensate people to visit their stores as mystery shoppers? Other companies pay people to call their customers and prospective customers. Families pay people to water their plants while they are on vacation or away on business. Babysitting is one of the oldest businesses, and something even teens can do.

I have a friend who has a challenged background and therefore has a hard time getting a job. But he is a husband and a father and is committed to providing for his family. He loves to clean cars. He has started a mobile car wash-equipped with water and all of the tools he needs to wash, detail, and make a car look brand new. He will bring his truck to your car wherever you may be. He can earn hundreds of dollars a day cleaning cars. And when he adds a few more trucks, he will be able to train young men to do what he does and earn a thousand dollars a day cleaning cars!

I also read about a woman who saved her house from foreclosure by baking cakes and selling them to her neighbors and friends. This effort turned into a full-fledged business and now she sells to people all across the country.

The key is to remain focused on our financial health and settle for nothing less than financial success.

Barriers or Obstacles: I have discovered that I can identify areas that are important to my financial goal:

1. I have discovered I have a weakness for ________________________________.
2. I have discovered I can potentially increase my income by ____________________.
3. I have discovered ________________________ is a very helpful person to hold me accountable to my new lifestyle __________________________.

Scripture and Practical Living: "I press on toward the goal…" (Philippians 3:14a, NIV).

Share how this Scripture is a support to you as you work through your barriers or obstacles.

____

____

II. BEGINNING TO BREAK AND ELIMINATE THE FINANCIAL CHAINS

Review Key Term(s):

Predatory lending – Unscrupulous actions carried out by a lender to entice, induce and/or assist a borrower in taking a mortgage that carries high fees, a high interest rate, strips the borrower of equity, or places the borrower in a lower credit rated loan to the benefit of the lender. (Investopedia, 3/2/13, www.investopedia.com/terms/p/predatory_ lending.asp).

Payday loans – a type of short-term, high interest loans based on your income (investopedia.com/terms/p/payday-loans.asp)

Net worth – The value of the assets a person or corporation owns, minus the liabilities they owe (investopedia.com/terms/n/networth.asp)

SUGGESTION BOX **Highlight the Key Term(s) or create an activity using the Key Terms**

Information and Statistics

- There are an estimated 10 million "shopaholics" in the United States who can't resist the temptation of using credit cards (American Journal of Psychiatry).
- Twelve million Americans are trapped every year in a cycle of 300% interest payday loans (Center for Responsible Lending).

Activity and Exercises

Claude and Grace wanted the family to enjoy themselves. How could they have lost so much money with only some cheap souvenirs to show for their time together? The children had fun, but Claude and Grace really felt cheated. They decided to stop complaining and enjoy their time with the kids and each other. Yet, they both kept thinking of the bills they could have paid had they waited until the fall to take the vacation, like the travel agent advised. The deals would've been much greater then.

Let's do some investigating and see if we can find out what might be the cause of the couple's problems, then provide them with some solutions to help. In helping them, we may even help ourselves or someone else we know. Reread their story and answer the following questions. You can do this individually or in groups:

- List possible reasons why Claude and Grace were emotionally upset:

1.____

2.____

3.____

- Write two strategies that will help Claude and Grace listen when others are giving them advice:

1.____

2.____

- Create two financial goals for Claude and Grace when planning vacations or other activities:

1.____

2.____

3.____

Share your answers with the class. If you are working through the process by yourself, discuss with someone who is part of the **dfree®** ministry whom you trust or ask a close friend to review your response.

As I analyzed Claude and Grace's financial problems, I realized that I can provide help for others, and apply this to myself. Maybe Claude, Grace, and I, (________ first name) can benefit from some positive changes in my actions, thoughts, and feelings. Therefore, I will repeat the dfree® Affirmation statements of encouragement to myself. (Look in the mirror and repeat the dfree® Affirmation statements.)

dfree® Affirmation

1. I am bombarded with messages designed to help me behave against my self-interest.
2. If I make mistakes, I can recover.
3. I have made financial progress already.

III. VICTORY STORY

"I wish I had known that I should not co-sign for someone's loan. I will never do it again."

- D.V.

IV. COMMITMENTS AND ASSIGNMENT(S)

Review and complete the following assignments before you begin the next session.

Commitments: As a result of my discovery, I commit to the following actions:

Commitment #1: My goal is to increase my income by $ ______ per month.

Commitment #2: I will make a list of things I love to do or do well enough to get people to pay me for it:

1.____

2.____

3.____

4.____

Commitment #3: With my new income, I am committed to increasing my savings or debt re- duction by $ ______ per month.

Commitment #4: I will log-on to the Billion Dollar Challenge's website (www. billiondollarpaydown.com) and increase my debt reduction goals.

Commitment #5: I will update my personal financial statement using the chart below:

What is my net worth now?

As I continue my journey to become debt-free and pay off my debts, my net worth should increase. Periodically calculating my net worth is one way to measure and track my financial status.

ASSETS (what you own)	VALUE
Personal Possessions	
Home value	
2nd home value	
Car	
Art, collectibles,jewelry, furniture	
Other	
Savings and Investments	
Cash on-hand	
Bank accounts	
CDs	
Annuities	
Life insurance cash value	
Stocks	
Bonds	
Mutual funds	
Real estate	
Retirement Savings	
Pension plan	

LIABILITIES (what you owe)	VALUE
Personal Debts	
Home loan	
2nd home loan	
Home equity loan	
Car loan	
Student loan	
Credit Cards + Personal Loans	
Visa	
Master Card	
American Express	
Other credit card	
Personal loans	
Unpaid bills	
Income tax owed	
Other debt	
Investment Debt	
Business loan	
Investment loan	

401(k)s	
IRAs	
SEPs	
Other	
TOTAL ASSETS	

401(k) loan	
Life insurance loan	
Other	
TOTAL LIABILITIES	
TOTAL ASSETS	
TOTAL LIABILITIES	
NET WORTH (Assets – Liabilities)	

Remember: My net worth ≠ My self-worth!

Commitment #5 (continued): I will make a daily appointment with myself (for at least seven minutes) to continue to keep my **dfree®** commitments for my own financial freedom at ______:______ am/pm

Commitment #6: I will spend at least seven minutes every day on a personal financial matter.

Commitment #7: I will attend the next **dfree®** session on ______ at ______.

Benefits: As a result of keeping my commitments, my life will be better in the following ways:

1.______________________________

2.______________________________

3.______________________________

V. HOME ASSIGNMENTS: Read chapter ten, "Invest in Others" in the **dfree®** book.

Answer the following after you have had a moment to reflect on the class, your situation, and pray. Responsible Actions I need to schedule and do this week:

____

____

Closing prayer: *"God, help me to remember that my identity is in You and if I resist the devil, he will flee from me. Amen."*

Resources:

Investopedia.com paydayloaninfo.org responsiblelending.org

dfree® Lifestyle

LEVEL FOUR – GIVE BACK

STEP TEN – INVEST IN OTHERS

Opening prayer: *"Dear God, You said that the truly great among us would serve. Give me a servant spirit and help me set at least one captive free. Amen."*

Response: Others have helped me with my financial journey. Now it is time for me to help others with their journey.

LIFE SITUATION – READ AND ANSWER THE QUESTION(S) BELOW: Reaching Out to Others

Jacob and Joshua were doing well in their music and video business. They worked well together and complemented each other. Joshua had a strong business sense and Jacob was very good at marketing and selling their products. Each had a wonderful singing voice and they could play the piano, drums, and other instruments after hearing a song just once. Reading music and adding their own interpretation added a soulful and fun flavor to their sound. Their sisters assisted with costumes and writing songs—especially Taylor—and whatever else they could add. Saving and investing in the business was going well. Some of their friends wanted to know the details of starting a business and their financial success. Joshua and DJ began a small group for young people ages 16-21 who wanted to learn about financial freedom. Their brothers and sisters assisted as needed. Although Grace and Claude were grateful and excited about the "family" business, they couldn't help but think what if…

Let's see if we can think about what concerns Grace and Claude might have and why the siblings are successful. In helping them, we may even help ourselves or someone else we know. Reread their story and answer the following questions. You can do this individually or in groups:

- List possible reasons why Grace and Claude are concerned:

1.______________________________

2.______________________________

3.______________________________

- Write two challenges that might cause tension or problems for the family businesses:

1.______________________________

2.____

- Create two financial goals for the siblings:

1.____

2.____

I. UNCOVERING THE CHAINS

Our session today is about investing in others. The goal of this session is to help others achieve financial freedom.

Memory Verse: "For where your treasure is, there your heart will be also" (Matthew 6:21, NIV).

Reflect and share with someone why you think Jesus said this. Are His words true in your life today and how?

____

____

A FINANCIAL STRONGHOLD MESSAGE FROM DR. SOARIES:

Jesus was God in the flesh. Yet Jesus got on His knees and washed His followers' feet. After He washed their feet, He instructed them to wash each others' feet. He said that if He was the master and if He could wash their feet, they, as His disciples, could wash each other's feet. For Jesus service was part and parcel of being His disciple and follower (John 13:1-17 NIV).

Harriet Tubman was born a slave in 1820. In 1849, Tubman escaped to Philadelphia then im- mediately returned to Maryland to rescue her family. After escaping from slavery, she made 13 missions to rescue more than 70 slaves using a network of antislavery activists and safe houses known as the Underground Railroad. Slowly, one group at a time, she brought relatives out of the state and eventually guided dozens of other slaves to freedom. Traveling by night, "Moses," as she was called) "never lost a passenger." Large rewards were offered for the return of many fugitive slaves, but no one knew that Tubman was the one helping the slaves escape. When the federal government passed laws that required law officials in Free states to aid efforts to recapture slaves, Tubman helped guide escaped slaves further north to Canada, where slavery was prohibited.

Harriet Tubman was a role model for people who managed to break free. Her actions suggest that one is not truly free until one has helped someone else be free.

It does not always require a huge act. What may seem like a very small contribution could have a life-changing impact on another. I remember helping an elderly farmer in Jamaica buy a mule so he could expand his one-acre yam farm. He was saving to give his grandson $175 to buy a mule. With that mule, he could double his harvest and increase his annual income from $700 to $1400. It would take years for the farmer and his son to save $175, given the limitations of his $700 annual income. I had traveled to Jamaica with four friends and the exchange rate was five Jamaican dollars to one U.S. dollar. That meant that if we each gave the farmer $7, he could buy his mule immediately and not wait the 30 or 40 years he had expected. That is exactly what we did. We gave the man $7 US each—and he had 175 Jamaican dollars to buy his mule. We never missed the $7 we gave, but the farmer's life was changed forever.

Research has revealed that we are actually happier when we give to others. Therefore, giving is good for our health! Giving is a joy. That includes giving at least 10% of our income (tithing) to God through our church and supporting our favorite educational, civic organization or charitable organization.

Barriers or Obstacles: I have discovered that I can invest in others in the following ways:

1.____

2.____

3.____

Scripture and Practical Living: "... see that you also excel in this grace of giving" (from 2 Corinthians 8:7, NIV).

Share how this Scripture is a support to you as you work through your barriers or obstacles.

____

____

II. BEGINNING TO BREAK AND ELIMINATE THE FINANCIAL CHAINS

Review Key Term(s):

Give Back – Sharing with others through the various resources you have including knowledge, money, clothing, food, kindness, etc.

Tithing – 10% of our income.

SUGGESTION BOX **Highlight the Key Term(s) or create an activity using the Key Terms**

Information and Statistics:

- In 2013, Americans gave more than $358.38 billion to their favorite charities (Giving USA 2014: American Association of Fundraising Counsel).

Activity and Exercises

Joshua's New Life

Joshua did well in the music and video business. He had plans for his future and for his future family. Yet there are some things Joshua may not have planned for that you may be able to help him consider.

He was in his final year of college and was planning on attending grad school then purchase a house immediately after. His scholarship had become a full scholarship with a stipend. He still worked part time with the music and video company. In his junior year of college, Joshua had received a fellowship for research about the risk of alcohol and drugs in African American males between the ages of 25-35. Grad school was already paid for and he had another stipend waiting for him.

Joshua knew how to use his skills to help others, make money, and save money. He was a rare young man. He was goal-oriented and a hard worker. Joshua planned to marry his girlfriend, Gail, in two years. He hoped to have enough saved to make a large down payment—if not half—on a house he could rehab or buy out of foreclosure. He had learned how to do carpentry work and other handy work around the house from his father. Joshua also had friends who knew how to refurbish homes. Although Joshua had great plans, he had to refocus his attention since Gail was now pregnant with twins. He continued to enact his plan, but now he had to include Gail and the twins sooner. Joshua knew he had to make even more sacrifices, but at least he did not have to start off being in debt. He already knew he would teach his children the value of money and how to be financially responsible. Once they were born, he would set up trust funds for both of them.

Let's see if we can assist Joshua as he plans for his new life. Are there any obstacles or concerns that may impact his financial planning and other facts of his new life? What are the joys he can draw from if a need does arise? As we look at Joshua's life, we may even help ourselves or someone else we know. Reread his story and answer the following questions. You can do this individually or in groups:

- List possible reasons why Joshua should be concerned:

1.____

2.____

3.____

- Write two challenges that might cause problems for Joshua and Gail:

1.____

dfree® Affirmation

1. I can help someone who is struggling with his or her finances.
2. I don't have to be a financial expert to help someone become **dfree®**.
3. The best way to sustain my own progress is to help someone learn what I have leaned and experience what I have experienced.

2.____

- Create two financial goals for Joshua:

1.____

2.____

Share your answers with the class. If you are working through the process by yourself, discuss with someone who is part of the **dfree®** ministry whom you trust or ask a close friend to review your response.

As I analyzed the children's concerns, I realized that I can provide help for others, and apply this to myself. Maybe Jacob, Joshua, DJ, Taylor, and Stacey, and I (________ first name), can benefit from some positive changes in my actions, thoughts, and feelings. Therefore, I will repeat the dfree® Affirmation statements of encouragement to myself. (Look in the mirror and repeat the dfree® Affirmation statements.)

III. VICTORY STORY

"dfree® taught me how to give and how to spend wisely. The best way to be able to give is when you're financially free. Someone asked me one time, "Well you're already debt free, why would you want to go take a class?" I know there is so much more I can learn, and I can give back and show others how to become **dfree®."**

- Patricia

IV. COMMITMENTS AND ASSIGNMENT(S)

Review and complete the following assignments before you begin the next session.

Commitments: As a result of my discovery, I commit to the following actions:

Commitment #1: I will share what I have accomplished during this **dfree®** lifestyle workbook with the following people:

1.______________________________

2.______________________________

3.______________________________

4.______________________________

5.______________________________

Commitment #2: I will invite the following friends and family members to join the **dfree®** Billion Dollar Challenge, www.billiondollarpaydown.com, to set and track their debt reduction goals and progress:

1.______________________________

2.______________________________

3.______________________________

4.______________________________

5.______________________________

Commitment #3: I will support ________ with a minimum of ________% of my income.

Commitment #4: I will give the following people some type of assistance or gift that will help them reach their financial goals.

1.______________________________

2.______________________________

3.______________________________

4.______________________________

Commitment #5: I will make a daily appointment with myself (for at least seven minutes) to continue to keep my **dfree®** commitments for my own financial freedom at ________:________ am/pm

Commitment #6: I will contact ________________ when I begin to stray from my previous **dfree®** commitments.

Commitment #7: I will attend the next **dfree®** session on _______ at _______.

Benefits: As a result of keeping my commitments, my life will be better in the following ways:

1.____________________

2.____________________

3.____________________

V. HOME ASSIGNMENTS:

Read chapter eleven, "Ignite **dfree®** Living" in the **dfree®** book. Answer the following after you have had a moment to reflect on the class, your situation, and pray. Responsible Actions I need to schedule and do this week:

Closing prayer: *"God, thank You for the blessing of being able to give what I have learned and experienced to someone else. Amen."*

Resources:

Crown.org

dfree® Lifestyle

LEVEL FOUR – GIVE BACK

STEP ELEVEN – IGNITE DFREE® LIVING

Opening prayer: *"Dear God, I still have so many plans, dreams, and goals. Help me remember that I can be a blessing to others, even while I am working on myself. Amen."*

Response: Each one teach one.

LIFE SITUATION – READ AND ANSWER THE QUESTION(S) BELOW: New Beginnings

Claude and Grace could not believe it! Not Joshua! How could he? Maybe Jacob, DJ, or Taylor could possibly have done this, but not Joshua. Well, it was done, and everyone had to deal with it and move on in ways that would be best for all involved. Is there anything you can learn from

Joshua?

____

____

I. UNCOVERING THE CHAINS

Our session today is about giving back to others. The goal of this session is to assist others in their journey toward financial freedom.

Memory Verse: "The Spirit of the Lord is on me, because he has anointed me to proclaim good news to the poor. He has sent me to proclaim freedom for the prisoners and recovery of sight for the blind, to set the oppressed free" (Luke 4:18 NIV).

Reflect and share with someone why you think Jesus said this. Are His words true in your life today? How?

____

____

A FINANCIAL STRONGHOLD MESSAGE FROM DR. SOARIES:

Start a movement! In our memory verse, Jesus launches His ministry by using the words of Isaiah to describe His mission: good news for the poor, freedom for prisoners, sight for the blind, and freedom for the oppressed. As the body of Christ, the Church has the same calling and mission. Every Christian who shares in this mission will contribute to a movement that improves life for others.

Movements are started by ordinary people. People like Dr. Martin Luther King, Jr. possess unusual gifts that cause them to stand out from the crowd. Dr. King's ability to speak was unique. But the Civil Rights Movement did not start with Dr. King's speeches. He became known as a great speaker because an ordinary woman named Rosa Parks refused to move when a bus driver told her to give up her seat to a white passenger. Mrs. Parks was an ordinary, quiet, African American woman. She was a seamstress, a church organist, and a devoted wife. But her action became the spark of a movement that changed America forever.

The commitment to help people resist the forces of consumerism and take care of his or her financial health is as urgently needed today as was the need to achieve Civil Rights in the 1960s. The only way to reach the vast number of people who need to hear our message is for ordinary people to become as a movement. Most people cannot speak like Dr. King, but everyone can take a stand like Mrs. Parks. She proved that one ordinary person's action can inspire others to take extraordinary action.

Barriers or Obstacles: I have discovered the following about myself through the **dfree®** experience:

1. I have discovered that I would not be where I am today were it not for ______________.

2. I am so grateful for the help I have received that I plan to __________________________.

3. This **dfree®** experience has been particularly helpful to me in the area of ______________.

Scripture and Practical Living: "You, my brothers [and sisters] are called to be free. But do not use your freedom to indulge the sinful nature, rather, serve one another in love" (Galatians 5:13, NIV).

Share how this Scripture is a support to you as you work through your barriers or obstacles.

____

____

II. BEGINNING TO BREAK AND ELIMINATE THE FINANCIAL CHAINS

Review Key Term(s):

Movement – "a large group of people who make a collective effort to achieve something, especially a political or social reform" (merriam-webster.com/dictionary/movement).

Information and Statistics:

- About 62.6 million Americans, gave 7.8 billion hours of volunteer service worth $184 billion in 2015 (Corporation for National and Community Service).

Activity and Exercises

Doing Things Differently: Because of the change in Joshua and Gail's life, Joshua, Gail, and the family need to work together to stay focused financially and spiritually. Claude and Grace were great parents, but they were surprised. Gail's parents were disappointed, but supported their daughter. Joshua was a planner and a hard worker. Gail was organized and worked hard, too. They would need help whether they knew it or not.

Let's see how the families can work together to assist Joshua and Gail. Are there any family obstacles or concerns that may impact their getting married and raising a family together? How can the families work through their disappointments and keep financially focused? As we look at the families, we may even help ourselves or someone else we know. Reread the story and answer the following questions. You can do this individually or in groups:

SUGGESTION BOX **Highlight the Key Term(s) or create an activity using the Key Terms**

- List possible reasons why the family may be disappointed in Joshua and Gail:

1.____

2.____

3.____

- Write two challenges that may cause obstacles for the family financially:

1.____

2.____

- Create one short-term and one long-term financial goal for Joshua and Gail:

1.____

2.____

Share your answers with the class. If you are working through the process by yourself, discuss with someone who is part of the **dfree®** ministry whom you trust or ask a close friend to review your response.

As I analyzed Joshua, Gail, and the families' financial problems, I realized that I can provide help for others, and apply this to myself. Maybe Joshua, Gail, and I, (________ first name) can benefit from some positive changes in my actions, thoughts, and feelings. Therefore, I will repeat the dfree® Affirmation statements of encouragement to myself. (Look in the mirror and repeat the dfree® Affirmation statements.)

III. VICTORY STORY

"Clearly, Dr. Soaries is onto something with the **dfree®** movement. I heard him speak at a training conference and it astonished me how much sense he made as he used statistics to reveal the bad habits we often refuse to admit. The whole time I'm sitting there thinking about how we can incorporate **dfree®** into our organization. I will recommend having Dr. Soaries come in and train a core leadership group. Then we hit it hard with putting on these types of no-nonsense training seminars around the communities.

We can explain what it means to be constrained by debt and how we're weighed down by all those other bad financial bad habits we cling to, such as using those check-cashing places, not having checking or saving accounts, carrying balances on multiple credit cards, not having life insurance, not monitoring our credit reports, and not making payments on time. The list goes on and on…I see a vision here for a new way of life that can set so many people free to really live for the first time in their adult lives."

- Thom

dfree® Affirmation

1. I can improve the way I handle my personal business.
2. It helps me to be challenged to take action.
3. I need to stop thinking about changing and actually do something about change.

IV. COMMITMENTS AND ASSIGNMENT(S)

Review and complete the following assignments before you begin the next session.

Commitments: As a result of my discovery, I commit to the following actions:

Commitment #1: I will contact the following organizations or groups and encourage them to include **dfree®** in their activities:

1. ____

2. ____

3. ____

Commitment #2: I believe the following members of my family could benefit from **dfree®** instruction:

1.____

2.____

3.____

Commitment #3: I will spend ________ hours a week helping someone reach their **dfree®** goals.

Commitment #4: I will promote **dfree®** in the following ways:

1.____

2.____

3.____

4.____

5.____

Commitment #5: I will form a group in the Billion Dollar Challenge (www.billiondollarpaydown.com) and lead them to adopt a **dfree®** Lifestyle.

Date formed: _______________ Group name: _______________

Commitment #6: I will promote **dfree®** living using the following social media platforms:

1.____

2.____

3.____

4.____

Commitment #7: I will attend the next **dfree®** session on ___________ at ____________.

Benefits: As a result of keeping my commitments, my life will be better in the following ways:

1.____

2.____

3.____

V. HOME ASSIGNMENTS: Read chapter twelve, "Impact the Culture" in the **dfree®** book.

Answer the following after you have had a moment to reflect on the class, your situation, and pray. Responsible Actions I need to do and say this week:

____

____

Closing prayer: *"Lord, thank You for the opportunity to serve. Amen."*

Resource:

dfreefoundation.org

dfree® Lifestyle

LEVEL FOUR – GIVE BACK

STEP TWELVE – IMPACT THE CULTURE

Opening prayer: *"Dear God, I still have so many plans, dreams, and goals. Help me remember that I can be a blessing to others, even while I am working on myself. Amen."*

Response: If it is to be, it is up to me.

LIFE SITUATION – READ AND ANSWER THE QUESTION(S) BELOW: Time for a Change

Claude and Grace worked through their problems. Not always in the best way, but they learned how to respect one another and figure things out together. Financially, things had begun to settle down for the family. They were not buying just to buy and they'd stopped giving away things only to purchase the same item again at a higher price. Both Claude and Grace learned to appreciate what they had. They also learned that it is necessary to help others and teach your own children and family to be responsible and accountable in all areas of their lives.

Claude and Grace were thankful for their parents, children, family, friends, church, and their relationship with the Lord. Claude and Grace knew they had to practice what they preached so the people around them could see, through their actions, that they both believed what they said. It was difficult at times, but rewarding in the long run. Claude and Grace are both leaders in a **dfree®** com- munity program that meets at the church and at the local community center. One day, with Joshua's assistance, they would like to start a **dfree®** program for children and youth.

Share why you think Claude and Grace want to share their **dfree®** living with others? What approaches might they take with people who are opposed to what they have to say?

____

____

I. UNCOVERING THE CHAINS

Our session today is about impacting the culture. The goal of this session is to make a difference in the financial lives within our society.

Memory Verse: "Two are better than one, because they have a good return for their work: If one falls down, his friend can help him up. But pity the man who falls and has no one to help him up!" (Ecclesiastes 4:9-10 NIV).

Reflect and share with someone why do you think the writer said this. Are his words true in your life today and how?

____

____

A FINANCIAL STRONGHOLD MESSAGE FROM DR. SOARIES:

This is what the jealous leaders said about Paul and Silas in the city of Thessalonica after they arrived: "These men who have caused trouble all over the world have now come here…" (Acts 17:6). Christians are called upon to be more than good people. We have been called to make a difference. The ministry of Paul and Silas did more than inspire the church - they actually disturbed the city!

Our economic systems that allow us to be overtaken by consumerism and conditions that prey upon so many vulnerable people cry out for some "disturbances." The values that have become embedded in our culture are so different than the teachings of Jesus that we need Christians who are willing to change the culture. That includes the culture of debt.

We live in the fastest-changing period of human history. Something significant in our culture changes every 18 months! Everyone can identify something that is different now than it was two years ago. We are moving at lightning speed.

Barriers or Obstacles: I have discovered that I feel a need to help combat the culture of ______________________ by ______________________

Scripture and Practical Living:

"And do not forget to do good and to share with others, for with such sacrifices God is" (Hebrews 13:16, NIV).

Share how this Scripture is a support to you as you work through your barriers or obstacles.

____

____

II. BEGINNING TO BREAK AND ELIMINATE THE FINANCIAL CHAINS

Review Key Term(s): The following terms are explained in detail under Activity and Exercises

Culture of greed   Culture of impatience   Culture of ignorance

Culture of fantasy
Culture of denial
Culture of victimhood
Culture of prosperity

SUGGESTION BOX **Highlight the Key Term(s) or create an activity using the Key Terms**

Information and Statistics:

- 41% of U.S. adults-more than 2 million people-gave themselves a grade of C, D, or F on their knowledge of personal finance, suggesting there is considerable room for improvement. This number is highest among Gen Y adults at 47%. 80% of adults agree they would benefit from advice and answers to everyday financial questions from a professional, and more than one-third (35%) strongly agree. (National Foundation for Credit Counseling)

Activity and Exercises

The culture of debt, the lack of savings, and self-imposed poverty is a relatively new (less than 50 years) societal challenge characteristic of our society. However, this culture did not create itself or grow in a vacuum. The culture of debt is actually the offspring of seven other cultures produced by their interactions and interactivities. Our efforts to sustain and spread the **dfree®** Lifestyle involve addressing all of these other cultures:

1. The Culture of Greed

During the 1980s, greed caused banks to offer high interest rate credit cards and mortgages to people who were not able to afford them. It is greed that allows corporations to dole out huge bonuses to executives while freezing wages and cutting jobs for low-wage workers. It is greed that motivates clothing designers to charge exorbitant prices for apparel made overseas in sweatshops, or assign higher prices simply due to the presence of a logo. It is greed that causes payday lenders to prey upon people of meager means, offering them access to credit that can result in repayment interest rates of 400 to 800%. And not all of this culture of greed resides in corporate suites.

The culture of greed also causes people to abandon family responsibilities to work more hours and earn more money to buy more things. Greed is at work when we buy more clothes than we can wear, store them in basements and attics, and then rent storage units to house things we may never use again. We have replaced the cultures of modesty, sufficiency, and frugality with the culture of greed. When this culture interacts with one of the other cultures detailed here, it produces the culture of debt.

2. The Culture of Impatience

No longer do we have a culture of delayed gratification, where we are willing to wait for an item we want until we can pay for it. We have become a plastic society. We used to make payments for a purchase before we obtained it. Now we obtain the item and then we make the payments over time. In my mother's time, there were no interest charges with layaway. But now when we "charge it," we pay high interest rates that diminish our buying power. This inability to wait has not only affected our finances, it has permeated our entire existence. We cannot wait for food, so we want fast food. We cannot wait at traffic signals, so we have road rage. We cannot even wait to discover the gender of our children. We are addicted to fast and cannot tolerate any type of delays-especially with those things we think make us happy or bring us joy. Since our greatest happiness is perceived to be in our possessions, we cannot wait until we can afford them. We will pay 14%-28% interest rates on credit cards to have what we want right away.

3. The Culture of Ignorance

In the U.S., we seem to be comfortable with a culture of ignorance as if ignorance really is bliss. We have been completely distracted by frivolity and foolish things that just don't matter. In some cases, we have no grasp or interest in matters related to our own welfare. In the **dfree®** program, we discovered that many people did not know the interest rates they were paying on their car loans. Most of the people we asked admitted they were only interested in the amounts of their monthly payments and never thought about interest rates. There is an old expression: "What you don't know won't hurt you." The truth is, what we don't know can kill us. It has be- come acceptable to know more about celebrities' lives than our own.

State-sponsored lotteries are the worst of example of government capitalizing on the cultures of greed, impatience, and ignorance. The odds of becoming rich by winning a lottery are beyond anything reasonable. Yet Americans spend $80 billion a year on state-sponsored lottery tickets. In one city families with yearly earnings of $13,000 spend an average of $645 a year or $53.75 per month on lottery tickets. That monthly expenditure is 5% of their annual income! A monthly deposit of $53.75 in an account that yields 5% interest will result in their having $22,238.86 in 20 years!

4. The Culture of Fantasy

Celebrity worship depicts a culture of fantasy that has allowed make-believe to become our reality. Professor Juliet B. Schor has analyzed this in a marvelous way in her book, "The Over- spent American." She asserts that in the past, striving for improved lifestyles was not totally negative because the Joneses lived next door to us and were probably in the same income bracket and had similar lifestyles. But today, we don't even know the Joneses who we are trying to keep up with. And all too often we idolize film and television characters that make a lot more money than we earn and even worse, who don't exist.

This fantasy-based culture offers emotional and psychological support to misplaced priorities and processes. Like millions of kids who really believe they will play professional basketball and therefore do not need an education, millions of families believe some miracle will occur that will enable them to pay bills for which they lack money. Their purchases make them feel like they are a part of the world they can imagine, and thus their debt facilitates their fantasy.

5. The Culture of Denial

We are living in a constant state of denial about so many things that one wonders if there is not really an epidemic of undiagnosed mental illness. We are in denial about our children and their behavior. We are in denial about our health and what is required of us to be healthy. And we are in complete denial about our finances and how to be financially healthy.

6. The Culture of Victimhood

If we are not careful, everyone will be able to identify some way in which they are victims of someone else's actions. Granted, there is no limit to the number of schemes designed to take advantage of and even hurt people. So many homeowners who signed ill-advised mortgage notes were either poorly represented or fraudulently represented. Many companies that purported to help struggling homeowners were actually criminal enterprises. That is why we must dedicate ourselves to understanding what we sign, securing professional advice, and asking questions when we don't know what we are doing. We cannot be too careful about protecting ourselves, our families, and our assets from rip-offs.

But not everything is a rip-off. Some of our problems are self-imposed and we must learn to take responsibility for what we do to ourselves. The culture of victimhood removes all personal responsibility and assigns blame for all of our problems on external sources.

If we do not open our mail and respond to letters that we get from lenders, when they repossess our cars or foreclose our homes, we are at fault. If we misrepresent the truth on applications, we are responsible. If we spend money on things we do not need and are unable to handle our regular responsibilities, we must accept the consequences.

7. The Culture of Prosperity

There was a time when purpose, significance, and service were celebrated as virtues worth pursuing and possessing. Instead, we have evolved into the culture of prosperity. We not only admire the "lifestyles of the rich and famous," we hold them up as the standard for significance and success. We believe, too, that we're so entitled to this standard that we'll lie, cheat, and refuse self-accountability just so we can claim prosperity as our own. Prosperity is often mistakenly and very narrowly defined as simply having money and possessions.

Prosperity certainly is not evil. But in a culture of prosperity social and spiritual status are based on possessions rather than integrity and accomplishment.

- List three reasons why you and others may live in a culture of denial:

1.______________________________

2.______________________________

3.______________________________

- Write two challenges that keep you and others living in a culture of fantasy:

1.____

2.____

- Decide on two areas you are most vulnerable to living in a culture of greed and what you will do starting__(date) to make a change and in the culture:

1.____

2.____

Share your answers with the class. If you are working through the process by yourself, discuss with someone who is part of the **dfree®** ministry whom you trust or ask a close friend to review your response.

I, (________ first name) can benefit from some positive changes in my actions, thoughts, and feelings. Therefore, I will repeat the dfree® Affirmation statements of encouragement to myself. (Look in the mirror and repeat the dfree® Affirmation statements.)

dfree® Affirmation	**1.** The best way to celebrate my personal victory is to serve others who need help. **2.** People achieve better results when they receive help from someone who has shared their experience. **3.** One person can make a difference that changes the culture.

III. VICTORY STORY

"I just received an email after spending over an hour with a young lady who heard your **dfree®** tele- phone presentation on insurance. She is so thankful that you took the time to share your knowledge and can't thank us enough for pointing out that she is not insured correctly on her condo.

... Her current policy was only providing $20,000 in coverage, which means she had an $80,000 shortage in the event of a loss. As a result of you volunteering your time and sharing what you know, she will be making the appropriate changes to her current policy and will be receiving quotes from [insurance] carriers to see where she can get the best coverage."

- Employee email to her supervisor at an insurance agency

IV. COMMITMENTS AND ASSIGNMENT(S)

Review and complete the following assignments before you begin the next session.

Commitments: As a result of my discovery, I commit to the following actions:

Commitment #1: I will participate in an activity that helps people with:

1.______________________________

2.______________________________

3.______________________________

Commitment #2: I will encourage people to avoid alternative financial services, such as:

1. Payday loans
2. Title loan store
3. Pawn shops
4. Check cashing stores
5. Tax refund anticipation loans
6. Overdraft protection loans
7. ______________________________

Commitment #3: I will support a ministry or organization that promotes financial literacy. Name of organization: ____________________

Commitment #4: I will subscribe to a resource that provides ongoing financial information. Name: ____________________

Commitment #5: I will celebrate someone else's progress with their **dfree®** Lifestyle. Name: ____________________

Commitment #6: I will develop a strategy to maintain my **dfree®** commitments after the **dfree®** sessions end.

Commitment #7: I will identify the next book I will read to expand my knowledge of personal finance. Title: ____________________

Benefits: As a result of keeping my commitments, my life will be better in the following ways:

1.______________________________

2.______________________________

3.____

V. HOME ASSIGNMENTS:

Celebrate with Thanksgiving and praising God! Go and share **dfree®** with others and stay **dfree®!**

Answer the following after you have had a moment to reflect on the class, your situation, and pray.

Responsible Actions I need to schedule and do this week:

____

____

Closing prayer: *"God, I thank You for my freedom. I could not have done this by myself. I promise to help someone make it to financial freedom in the same way someone helped me. Amen."*

Resource:

dfreefoundation.org

CONGRATULATIONS!

You have successfully completed dfree® Lifestyle: 12 Steps to Financial Freedom.

As our special gift, visit www.dfreefoundation.org to receive a free list of all the affirmations in this book in a printable format. Additionally, you will receive a **dfree®** Lifestyle: 12 Steps to Financial Freedom Completion Certificate in a printable format, suitable for framing.

GLOSSARY OF ONLINE RESOURCES

agingwithdignity.org

annualcreditreport.com

bankrate.com

billiondollarpaydown.com

consumerfinance.gov/credit-cards

consumerjungle.org

disabilitycanhappen.org

estateplanning.com

federalreserve.gov

financiallit.org

hud.gov

insurancecalculators.com

insure.com

investopedia.com

kiplinger.com

mint.com

money.strands.com

mymoney.com

nerdwallet.com

ownthedollar.com

paydayloaninfo.org

practicalmoneyskills.com

responsiblelending.org

NOTES

NOTES

NOTES

DeForest B. Soaries, Jr., D.Min.

Dr. Soaries is the President and CEO of Corporate Community Connections, Inc., a company that assists corporations expand and improve their Corporate Social Responsibility efforts. In July 2021 he retired from 30 years of ministry as the third Senior Pastor of First Baptist Church of Lincoln Gardens ("FBCLG") in Somerset, New Jersey. His pastoral ministry focused on spiritual growth, educational excellence, economic empowerment, and faith-based community development. As a pioneer of faith-based community development, Dr. Soaries' impact on FBCLG and the community was tremendous. In 1992, he founded the Central Jersey Community Development Corporation ("CJCDC"), a 501(c)(3) non-profit organization that specializes in helping revitalize underserved and vulnerable neighborhoods. In 1996, the CJCDC launched Harvest of Hope Family Services Network, Inc. This organization developed permanent solutions for hundreds of foster children and parents.

Dr. Soaries was inducted to the The Martin Luther King Jr Board of Preachers at Morehouse College.

From 1999 to 2002, Dr. Soaries served as New Jersey's Secretary of State, making him the first and only African-American male to serve in that office. He also served as the former chairman of the United States Election Assistance Commission, which was established by Congress to implement the "Help America Vote Act" of 2002.

In 2005, Dr. Soaries launched the dfree® Financial Freedom Movement. The dfree® strategy teaches people how to become financially self-sufficient. His work in financial empowerment was featured in a CNN documentary.

Dr. Soaries has written 12 books including "Say Yes to No Debt" and "Say Yes When Life Says No." he is the host of a weekly radio show "For Your Soul" on SiriusXM Urban View.

Dr. Soaries currently serves as an Independent Director at Independence Realty Trust and Ocwen Financial Corporation. He served as an Independent Director at the Federal Home Loan Bank of New York for 16 years. He also serves as a Trustee of RWJ Barnabas Health.

Soaries earned a Bachelor of Arts Degree from Fordham University, a Master of Divinity Degree from Princeton Theological Seminary, and a Doctor of Ministry Degree from United Theological Seminary. Dr. Soaries resides in Sarasota, Florida with his wife, Donna.

Made in the USA
Columbia, SC
09 February 2025